THE BEDFORD SERIES IN HISTORY AND CULTURE

The Discovery of Guiana

by Sir Walter Ralegh

WITH RELATED DOCUMENTS

Related Titles in
THE BEDFORD SERIES IN HISTORY AND CULTURE
Advisory Editors: Lynn Hunt, *University of California, Los Angeles*
David W. Blight, *Yale University*
Bonnie G. Smith, *Rutgers University*
Natalie Zemon Davis, *Princeton University*
Ernest R. May, *Harvard University*

THE BEDFORD SERIES IN HISTORY AND CULTURE

The Discovery of Guiana

by Sir Walter Ralegh

WITH RELATED DOCUMENTS

Edited with an Introduction by

Benjamin Schmidt

University of Washington

BEDFORD/ST. MARTIN'S   Boston ♦ New York

To Isabel, the boldest (and sweetest) explorer I know

For Bedford/St. Martin's

Executive Editor for History: Mary V. Dougherty
Director of Development for History: Jane Knetzger
Senior Developmental Editor: Sara Wise
Editorial Assistant: Laurel Damashek
Senior Production Supervisor: Joe Ford
Production Associate: Sarah Ulicny
Executive Marketing Manager: Jenna Bookin Barry
Project Management: Books By Design, Inc.
Text Design: Claire Seng-Niemoeller
Indexer: Books By Design, Inc.
Cover Design: Elizabeth Tardiff
Cover Art: Portrait of Sir Walter Raleigh, English, Artist Unknown. Oil on panel.
 25⅜" H × 19½" W. Inscribed upper right, *Sir Walter Raleigh Aetatis suae 36
 Anno Domini 1588.* Virginia Museum of Fine Arts, Richmond. Gift of Mrs. Preston
 Davie. Photo: Katherine Wetzel. © Virginia Museum of Fine Arts.
Composition: Stratford/TexTech
Printing and Binding: RR Donnelley & Sons Company

President: Joan E. Feinberg
Editorial Director: Denise B. Wydra
Director of Marketing: Karen Melton Soeltz
Director of Editing, Design, and Production: Marcia Cohen
Manager, Publishing Services: Emily Berleth

Library of Congress Control Number: 2007922532

Manufactured in the United States of America.

2 1 0 9 8 7
f e d c b a

For information, write: Bedford/St. Martin's, 75 Arlington Street, Boston, MA 02116
(617-399-4000)

ISBN-10: 0-312-15437-2
ISBN-13: 978-0-312-15437-0

Acknowledgments

Acknowledgments and copyrights are continued at the back of the book on
page 161, which constitutes an extension of the copyright page.

Foreword

The Bedford Series in History and Culture is designed so that readers can study the past as historians do.

The historian's first task is finding the evidence. Documents, letters, memoirs, interviews, pictures, movies, novels, or poems can provide facts and clues. Then the historian questions and compares the sources. There is more to do than in a courtroom, for hearsay evidence is welcome, and the historian is usually looking for answers beyond act and motive. Different views of an event may be as important as a single verdict. How a story is told may yield as much information as what it says.

Along the way the historian seeks help from other historians and perhaps from specialists in other disciplines. Finally, it is time to write, to decide on an interpretation and how to arrange the evidence for readers.

Each book in this series contains an important historical document or group of documents, each document a witness from the past and open to interpretation in different ways. The documents are combined with some element of historical narrative—an introduction or a biographical essay, for example—that provides students with an analysis of the primary source material and important background information about the world in which it was produced.

Each book in the series focuses on a specific topic within a specific historical period. Each provides a basis for lively thought and discussion about several aspects of the topic and the historian's role. Each is short enough (and inexpensive enough) to be a reasonable one-week assignment in a college course. Whether as classroom or personal reading, each book in the series provides firsthand experience of the challenge—and fun—of discovering, recreating, and interpreting the past.

Lynn Hunt
David W. Blight
Bonnie G. Smith
Natalie Zemon Davis
Ernest R. May

Preface

Sir Walter Ralegh lived large. He epitomized the energy, exuberance, and sheer drama of the Renaissance, and his story excellently demonstrates that the Renaissance was a global event, bridging the Atlantic and South American jungles no less than the British Isles. Ralegh's case also suggests that the history of European expansion needs revising and the clock of American history may need resetting. On the latter score, Ralegh's Guiana voyages and sponsorship of the Roanoke expeditions suggest a vital, late-sixteenth-century preamble to the traditional version of American history that focuses on the "foundational" settlement at Jamestown. As for European history, Ralegh's remarkable journey to the American tropics illustrates how open the competition over "discovery" and "new worlds" was at the time—how the Atlantic world readily mixed northern Europeans with Iberian rivals, indigenous Americans with European (and African) interlopers—and Ralegh's exceptional description of Guiana demonstrates one of the many ways early modern Europeans grappled with the otherness of their expanding universe. It also provides one of the few instances of a courtier-conquistador. Rare was the high-ranking royal favorite and gifted Renaissance poet found tramping around the equatorial jungles of America. Ralegh did it all, and *The Discovery of Guiana* stands out among encounter narratives both for the peerless grace of its author and the superbly crafted adventure it relates. The *Discovery* was justifiably popular in its day and has long ranked among the most important and enduring texts of European exploration.

Our understanding of Ralegh's adventure has shifted over time, and this volume seeks to incorporate into the classic history of English "discovery" the latest scholarship on Atlantic "encounters." There are several points of revision. First, whereas Ralegh has traditionally been studied in the context of Elizabethan politics and his voyages perceived in *opposition* to the Spanish *Conquista*, this volume juxtaposes Ralegh's deeds with those of his Iberian predecessors and presents

English activities as parallel to—rather than starkly different from—those of the Habsburg Empire. Ralegh is situated in his Elizabethan setting *and* the Atlantic world. Second, while earlier studies of the *Discovery* focused on high politics, passing in silence over its "fables" of Amazonian women and headless men, this edition integrates recent ethnographic scholarship on the indigenous populations of the Orinoco region, while also interrogating the production of "wonder" in early modern Europe. It takes seriously Ralegh's invocation of far-fetched exotica and contextualizes his efforts to understand the Indians. Third, while scholars have lately produced outstanding studies of Ralegh's poetry and prose, these two threads of literary criticism have not been adequately intertwined. The readings of the *Discovery* presented in this edition marshal formal insights gained from analyzing Ralegh's verse to shed new light on his prose narrative of exploration. This volume offers a fresh interpretation of the *Discovery* as an allegorical adventure: Ralegh performs a "courteous" conquest and endeavors in his actions—and prose—to improve on patterns of *Conquista*, thereby establishing a new model of American empire. That Ralegh failed is significant, of course, yet his narrative was a success all the same, and this edition probes the afterlife of the *Discovery* and its broad reception among European readers.

The introduction sets out these themes, offering an overview of the varied contexts of Ralegh and his American adventure. The first section, "Ralegh," provides a biography of the great Elizabethan courtier-conquistador, suggesting how the politics of the day would have induced his voyage of "courteous conquest." The second section, "Discovery," describes the development of European exploration and geographic wonder in the sixteenth century. It includes Spanish as well as English chapters of this story, situating Ralegh's Guiana quest in the wider world of Renaissance empire and expansion. The next section, on "Guiana," turns squarely to the Orinoco, its indigenous inhabitants, and European conceptions of the region—all in an effort to gauge what might have motivated Ralegh and his contemporaries when they risked their lives in search of El Dorado. The fourth section provides a close analysis of the text, exploring the literary themes and innovative forms deployed in the *Discovery*. It explains how Ralegh's narrative distinguished itself from other samples of travel literature and why it enjoyed such success. The epilogue considers the subsequent history of text and author: the reception of the *Discovery* after its publication, the historiography of Ralegh's considerable reputation, and the ultimate prospect of his "discoveries."

Ralegh's fame waxed and waned in his lifetime, and his Guiana voyage met with both skepticism and acclaim. The latter sentiment won the day, however, and Ralegh's *Discovery* gained immediate popularity. This edition explains why. It provides the essential text with other Ralegh writings—poetry as well as prose—and includes supplementary readings from early modern and medieval sources, particularly Spanish and English documents that elaborate on the themes of "discovery," *Conquista*, and European encounters with America. It includes visual sources, too, which offer the opportunity to assess Renaissance modes of self-fashioning and contemporary representations of Guiana and its natives. All of the documents include headnotes and explanatory glossary notes. Additional pedagogical elements include maps, a chronology of events, questions for consideration, and an annotated bibliography. Taken together, the sum of these parts presents a complete Ralegh's *Guiana*. This volume explores the themes of discovery and expansion, Renaissance culture and imperial politics, Atlantic-world rivalry and European-American encounters, and wonder and travel in an expanding world.

ACKNOWLEDGMENTS

My own voyage of Ralegh discovery has been extensive and enjoyable (more so than Ralegh's, I often imagine), and it is my pleasure to acknowledge the many who have helped along the way. Much of the research for this book was done at the Huntington Library, and I wish to thank Roy Ritchie for his support over the years and the excellent staff of the Reader Services Department. Also due thanks are the Andrew W. Mellon Foundation, the W. M. Keck Foundation, and the Royalty Research Fund of the University of Washington. Ronald Hoffman of the Omohundro Institute for Early American History and Culture invited me to present my Ralegh findings at a conference on Virginia and the Atlantic world, and this allowed me to work out ideas (published separately) on practices of reading Ralegh and early modern travel literature. Formative ideas came to fruition earlier in the process, too. I first encountered Ralegh's Guiana while teaching at Harvard's History and Literature Program, and I am pleased to have this chance to thank colleagues in those efforts, especially Sarah Cusk, who introduced me to Ralegh's poetry, and my earliest Ralegh mentor, Barbara Lewalski. Other colleagues and friends have been generous with their time and advice, including David Armitage, Scott

Black, Alan Gallay, Lynn Hunt, Peter Mancall, David Sacks, Paul Sellin, Andrew Wallace, Simon Werrett, and members of the Pacific Northwest Early Americanist Seminar. I am grateful, as well, for the reviewers, including Wayne Lee, University of Louisville; Peter Mancall, University of Southern California (who truly deserves this double thanks); Gayle Brunelle, California State University Fullerton; Jorge Cañizares-Esguerra, University of Texas; Jessica Kross, University of South Carolina; and Laura Stevens, University of Tulsa. I am very happy to acknowledge the enduring generosity and support of Chuck Christensen and Joan Feinberg of Bedford/St. Martin's. Mary Dougherty, Jane Knetzger, Shannon Hunt, Laurel Damashek, Nancy Benjamin, and Emily Berleth have all been helpful and encouraging when it came time to turn this project into a book. Sara Wise has been a wonderful editor; her professionalism has improved this book in numerous ways, for which I am most grateful. I am also fortunate to have an in-house editor of the skill and stature, grace and wisdom of Louise Townsend: to her I owe at least a voyage to the Caribbean, if not a jungle vacation up the Orinoco. Finally, to the *other* Queen Isabel—the explorer and conquistador of my home study—I dedicate this book with a twist on the royal proverb, uttered earlier of Isabel of Castile: As much as the queen takes away, she gives back even more.

Benjamin Schmidt

A Note about the Text

Walter Ralegh was an exact contemporary of William Shakespeare and, like the great bard, wrote in a form of English that may be challenging to twenty-first-century Americans. To render *The Discovery of Guiana* more accessible, I have modernized the spelling, adjusted the sometimes elaborate punctuation, and added paragraphs for clarity—yet otherwise kept much of the original form intact. I have been mindful, above all, of the rhythm of the text and tried to retain the author's strategic prose style. Ralegh composed the *Discovery* quickly and meant it to be read briskly as well; it was a polemic. The relatively new genre of travel literature, moreover, permitted a more relaxed form of composition, and Ralegh's generally vigorous narrative flows along with purposeful pauses and calibrated digressions. He meant, even with his punctuation, to persuade. That said, the punctuation and syntax of the *Discovery* differ notably from our own and can be confusing. Ralegh had a particular fondness for the comma and low regard for the period; his sentences can run for a whole paragraph, and I have broken these up. Ralegh sometimes makes use of parentheses as we do commas or dashes—to set apart passing thoughts or to record tangential events—yet sometimes does not. When these instances are not overly digressive, I have reworked them into the narrative with commas. Spelling has been uniformly updated, although I have retained the peculiar forms of some Spanish and indigenous American names (while correcting some commonly known Spanish personal names and place names) in order to illustrate the very weak grasp that even well-informed travelers such as Ralegh had of the Spanish Empire.

The notes mostly take the form of textual glosses, and for these I am indebted to the excellent, if perhaps less accessible, editions of Robert H. Schomburgk (1848) and V. T. Harlow (1928), both of which pay particular attention to the Spanish background of the voyage (on which Ralegh was strategically silent). For ethnographic data, I have also benefited from Neil Whitehead's edition. Readers who wish to consult the original, unedited version of the *Discovery* can easily do so in several rare book libraries and online. There is, finally, a new scholarly edition published by the Hakluyt Society and edited by Joyce Lorimer, which appeared too late for its findings to be incorporated into this edition.

Contents

PART THREE
Related Documents 113

Illustrations

THE BEDFORD SERIES IN HISTORY AND CULTURE

The Discovery of Guiana
by Sir Walter Ralegh

WITH RELATED DOCUMENTS

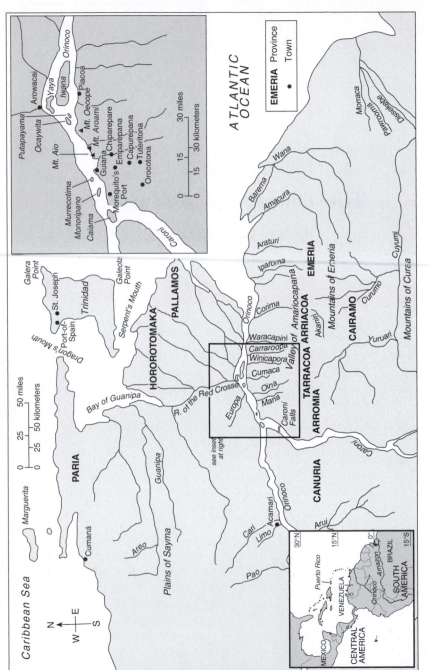

Contemporary Map of Guiana.

PART ONE

Introduction: Ralegh's Courteous Conquest

PROLOGUE: A PLASHY PLACE

Ralegh is a perfect reflection of the Renaissance imagination and a symbol of the English mind at a period when it was perhaps at its most alert and versatile.

Is it unreasonable to wonder whether Ralegh ever existed?[1]

The scene is London in the late sixteenth century; we are in the vicinity of the court. It is a pleasant enough day, though rain has been falling for the past few weeks, and England's greatest city is dank and muddy to its core. The queen is out for her morning stroll with her considerable entourage in tow: gay, if ostentatiously demure, ladies-in-waiting; soberly attired members of the Privy Council; young, vibrant, dashing courtiers. The royal person herself is the center of all attention, the focus of all gestures, the object of all blandishments: "Gloriana" in all her glory. The eldest daughter of Henry VIII, Queen Elizabeth presides over an ambitious island nation (the Spanish Armada would be routed in just a few years) and an aspiring imperial power. As a ruler, she is in her prime, and if no longer the fresh English beauty she was upon her coronation in 1558, she still cuts a striking figure and betrays a manner that is tellingly vain. The morning's outing is leisurely, the party's conversation urbane; yet the grubby path they follow is a wet, mucky disaster. "Urban jungle"

1

barely describes the rutted road by the Thames. The queen, in any event, is more than typically frustrated by the constant need to side-step, stretch over, and sometimes fully skip—an English queen!—over filthy pools of city sludge.

Enter our hero, among the more brightly decked young men angling for position and royal attention. He is known to dress brilliantly, and today is no exception. He once posed in "a white satin pinked vest, close-sleeved to the wrist, with a brown doublet finely flowered and embroidered with pearls, . . . a sword-belt, also brown and similarly decorated." (See Document 1, Figure 2.) He regularly dons one of several plumed hats embellished with rubies and pearl drops, along with white satin hose and gaily ribboned shoes. He is, in short, a clotheshorse. He also has a reputation for extravagant courage and bravery, most recently on display in the Anglo-Irish campaigns, where his military performance earned him wide acclaim. His goal today is more ambitious. As the queen comes to a particularly troublesome puddle—a "plashy place," as a chronicler famously put it—he springs into action: "Presently Ralegh cast and spread his new plush cloak on the ground, whereon the Queen trod gently, rewarding him afterward with many suits for his so free and seasonable tender of so fair a footcloth." Thus does Walter Ralegh enter the English court.[2]

Or so it is described in one of the most famous anecdotes handed down from Renaissance England. The story of Ralegh and his "plush cloak" tells us much about one of the greatest characters to occupy the stage of Elizabethan politics and, more generally, the operation of the early modern court. If the story is often dismissed as apocryphal—modern historians are quick to point out that the source of the tale did not witness those events he so charmingly describes—it reflects a common perception of Ralegh as a man of bold gestures.[3] Ralegh was known to be "free and seasonable," by which is meant that he acted with ostentatious generosity and a fine sense of timing. He was impulsive and a gambler—as the youngest son of a modest family, he had little choice—and the momentary sacrifice of a rich velvet coat was a calculated and opportune risk: nothing ventured, nothing gained. According to the chroniclers, Ralegh emerged that day as the queen's favorite. She admired his pluck and ingenuity, just as she would later admire his wit and debonair style. Yet with certain limits: Ralegh was always Elizabeth's "Water"—such was her pet name, a play on his broad Devonshire accent—and he never became one of the severely clad members of her inner circle. He was a performer on the court stage, yet never a policymaker or power broker. As a performer, he needed to improvise constantly to impress his fickle royal audience, and this meant a career of stylish gestures and high-risk gambles, some of which—such as his famous voyage to Guiana, the central act of his illustrious career—were far more reckless and costly than a plush cloak. And Ralegh's favor came and went like a sun-splashed London day: rain clouds were always on the horizon.

RALEGH, OR THE RENAISSANCE MAN IN FULL

Sir Walter Ralegh gives fresh, tangible meaning to the well-worn expression "Renaissance man." He led a spectacularly impressive and wide-ranging life, which touched upon virtually every facet of Elizabethan culture. "Authors are perplexed under what category to place him," wrote an early biographer who tried to do just that, "whether of statesman, seaman, soldier, chemist, or chronologer; for in all of these he did excel."[4] He did much more, too, with prodigious talents to match his immense ambitions. He was an admired poet (see Document 2), and he became one of England's most popular historians. He served as the preeminent sponsor of early English voyages to North America (he has been called the father of the British Empire, and it is Ralegh who christened the land "Virginia"), and he was an intrepid explorer of tropical South America. He conducted elaborate experiments in self-appointed laboratories, and he played a major part in turning back the vaunted Spanish Armada of 1588. He lived the classically Renaissance *vita activa* (active, political life) and *vita contemplativa* (contemplative, scholarly life), yet he did so in a manner that broke the boundaries between the two: "So contemplative was [Ralegh], that you would think he was not active; so active, that you would think that he was not prudent," opined a seventeenth-century biographer. "A great soldier, and yet an excellent courtier; an accomplished gallant, and yet a bookish man; a man that seemed born for anything he undertook."[5]

There is an irony to this final observation, since, in an important sense, Ralegh was hardly born to anything—and certainly not to the manor. He was the youngest son of Squire Walter Ralegh of Budleigh, a modestly prosperous gentleman from England's West Country (Devonshire), and his third and final wife, Katherine Gilbert. The future courtier and favorite of the queen entered the world nearly as low as one could go on early modern England's social totem pole. Family connections placed him among the "better sort," yet hardly above the rank of "a bare gentleman" (as he was once referred to disparagingly).[6] Ralegh's year of birth is uncertain but estimated to be 1554. We know very little about his youth; the first record of his life appears in the registers of Oriel College Oxford, where he enrolled in 1572 and likely stayed through 1574. Before his college stint, however, he spent time as a foot soldier in France, fighting for the Protestant cause in the ongoing (and bloody) French Wars of Religion (1562–1598). He may have ventured into the Low Countries as well, where the Calvinist-backed Dutch rebels had taken up arms against their Spanish Habsburg sovereign, Philip II. War, in all events, along with religious campaigns, occupied his mid-teens and left Ralegh with a taste for risk and adventure. It also solidified his strong Protestant leanings and impulsive dislike of Catholic Spain. He returned to England surely more seasoned than the average undergraduate and perhaps more easily bored by student life. Following Oxford, we find him in London at Lyons Inn (1574) and, soon after that, the Middle Temple (1575) — two institutions that were ostensibly meant to prepare young men for legal careers but that functioned more accurately as fashionable social clubs to foster political connections. His Protestant stirrings and academic impulses notwithstanding, the young Ralegh was on the make.

Making it in Elizabethan England, especially for someone of Ralegh's relatively modest background, demanded immense exertions. It also required the attention of patrons — powerful sponsors, generally with close ties to the court — which Ralegh vigorously sought in his early years. Throughout the 1570s, Ralegh exhibited a remarkable energy and restlessness; he broadened his range of activities and contacts to create as many openings for himself as possible. From the mid-1570s, he began to dabble in, then publish, poetry, which placed him in the circle of George Gascoigne, the most important poet of the day, and in contact with other leading literary figures of Elizabethan London, including Sir Philip Sidney.[7] In the winter of 1578–1579, Ralegh took part in a voyage of exploration with his half brother Sir Humphrey Gilbert in search of the Northwest Passage — the fabled northwesterly sea route from Europe to Asia. Although the expedition failed to get beyond the stormy waters of Plymouth, England, one ship braved the December gusts and ended up engaging a larger Spanish vessel, which earned the English ship's captain — Walter Ralegh — high marks for courage. Next came a tour of duty in Ireland, where Ralegh commanded a modest company of soldiers and led them — militarily successfully, if often quite brutally — against the

Figure 1. Sir Walter Ralegh *(ca. 1585), Nicholas Hilliard, miniature.*

Ralegh was renowned for his looks—tall, broad-shouldered, with thick curly hair and a wide forehead—an aspect he embellished with his sharp goatee and mustache. Despite its small dimensions, this miniature conveys the physical impressiveness of Ralegh, a quality enhanced by the extravagant lace, which would have been meant to catch the queen's eye.

National Portrait Gallery (NPG 4160), London. Watercolor on vellum, 48 mm × 41 mm.

local population resisting English rule. This led to a diplomatic mission to London, to deliver intercepted enemy letters, which was followed by yet another assignment in Ireland and then a second, triumphant return to London (1581) as a battle-hardened warrior. During these years, Ralegh was the model of vigor and motion, a rolling stone gathering momentum for bigger battles to come. In 1581, he arrived at the queen's court, a restless, dashing soldier none too covered in moss.[8]

If the anecdote of the queen and the "plashy place" may be untrue, there can be no doubt that Ralegh made a great splash upon his debut at the English court. Numerous factors worked in his favor—personal qualities that would have recommended him to the queen in particular and to court society more generally. First, and not insignificantly, Ralegh was considered very good-looking (Figure 1). Elizabeth certainly thought so, and it is striking how many of his biographers, from the early seventeenth century onward, seem to agree. The comments of Sir Robert Naunton are typical: "He had in the outward man a good presence, in a handsome and well-compact person, a strong natural wit and a better judgment, with a bold and plausible tongue, whereby he could set out his parts to the best advantage." A later observer rhapsodized over the young Ralegh as "slender but obviously muscular," conspicuously tall, and "a difficult man to miss." Ralegh dressed "flamboyantly," favoring large pearl earrings and lacy ruffs, and he famously "drank" tobacco from his ever-present clay pipe.[9] His conversational style was witty and sharp—sometimes even veering toward sarcastic—which made him the perfect foil for the overly formal, old-fashioned courtiers. He read widely and amassed an immense library of scholarly volumes, and he was reputed to sleep no more than five hours a night.[10] As do many smart, handsome, energetic bons vivants, Ralegh suffered from vanity: "He was a tall, handsome, and bold man," wrote the gossipy biographer John Aubrey, "but his *naeve* [blemish] was that he was damnable and proud."[11] Ralegh was above all a performer on the stage of Elizabethan politics, and he epitomized that quality of his day that the literary critic Stephen Greenblatt has labeled "Renaissance self-fashioning": the ability to project, or perform, a public persona, which in Ralegh's case meant the capacity to present himself as the embodiment of the daring, dynamic, and devoted courtier.[12]

Ralegh's climb was swift and dramatic. Whether with his plush cloak or bright wit, the handsome soldier with the Devonshire accent quickly gained the queen's favor and rose within the ranks of the court. When his military commander called him back to duty in Ireland in April 1582, the queen intervened to keep him at court, where he was to remain at her side, with few interruptions, for the better part of the decade. Elizabeth doted on her "Water"; he was her constant companion, her acknowledged favorite, and her trusty "oracle," as Ralegh's jealous competitors for the queen's attention put it. With this affection came rewards: state positions, royal honors, and, most straightforwardly, financial prizes. The latter took the form of patents from the crown, such as the right to collect taxes on the sale of wine, to receive custom duties on certain exported wools, and to control the tin-mining industry of the southwest counties of Ralegh's birth. Ralegh was elected to represent Devon in Parliament in 1584—he would hold that seat for the next two decades, except for the year of the Armada—and the queen knighted him in January of the following year. Over the subsequent months, Elizabeth effectively transformed

Ralegh from a modest-born soldier into the most powerful figure, after the queen, in the southwest corner of her realm, appointing him vice admiral for Devon and Cornwall, steward of the duchy of Cornwall, and lord lieutenant of Cornwall. She further granted him lands in Munster (southwest Ireland), and she placed at his disposal Durham House, one of the grandest residences in London. She showered him with jewelry. Finally, in 1587 the queen elevated Sir Walter Ralegh to captain of the guard, an honorary position that placed him at Elizabeth's beck and call, making him not only responsible for her physical protection but also privy to her every conversation, political decision, and courtly diversion. He was constantly at her side.

In return, Ralegh performed his role as favorite with energy and élan. The 1580s were Ralegh's decade; he was "the Queen's dear minion," as one court watcher put it, her charismatic and inseparable companion, and, by extension, the most powerful courtier of the realm.[13] Ralegh composed in these years some of his best poetry, almost all of it directed to the queen. He praised her beauty, wisdom, and grace; he bemoaned her distracted attention and fickle nature; he appealed for her lasting indulgence. Some of this verse may strike modern readers as clichéd and predictable: the pained lover pining for his beloved in sycophantic simile and otherwise baroque adulation. In truth, it reflects the mannered, Petrarchan style of the day, which was all the rage among Renaissance courtiers (in England as elsewhere); and if Ralegh did not innovate in his application of that style, he was more than adept in handling such verse. "He was sometimes a poet," as Aubrey deftly put it.[14] He was sometimes a scholar as well, and he famously supported a group of scientists (to use the modern word)—geographers, astronomers, alchemists, and mathematicians—who operated under his patronage. Again, this is less an example of innovation than application, and it suggests Ralegh's modus operandi. The Durham House set, as this group has been dubbed, debated, discussed, and sometimes demonstrated the latest examples of learning; and they converted Durham House, where Ralegh collected his many books and smart friends, into a fashionable spot to observe the finest minds of the realm. They did not so much produce knowledge as perform it.[15]

More dramatically—and perhaps more dynamically than such Renaissance garden-variety poetic efforts and scholarly displays—Ralegh took action. He sought and received patents for the discovery of foreign lands—the right to launch voyages to the New World—and this led to his sponsorship of the so-called Roanoke voyages. Here, too, Ralegh partly followed in the footsteps of others; his kinsman Sir Humphrey Gilbert had spent the late 1570s and early 1580s poking around the frigid waters of the North Atlantic in search of a quicker route to the Indies (South and East Asia). Yet the expeditions sponsored by Ralegh in the mid-1580s took a more southerly, uncharted, and frankly dangerous route to the heart of North America: present-day North Carolina and its environs, which lay perilously close to the Spanish settlement of Florida. Ralegh did not make any of these journeys himself, as the queen all but forbade him to leave her side. Yet he was the financial backer of the ships, energetic propagandist for the American enterprise, and titular governor, ultimately, of those lands henceforth to be called "Virginia." (In a bill introduced in the House of Commons, Ralegh took care also to note the native name newly bestowed on the English settlement, *Windgandcon* or *Wyngandacoia*, "which is as much to say as 'You wear good clothes.'")[16] By sponsoring these overseas ventures and then circulating news of his "discoveries," Ralegh may be said to have inaugurated England's imperial project in America. More to the point, he flattered the Virgin Queen, as Elizabeth allowed herself to be fashioned, with his performance (and canny sense of geographic nomenclature), and he gained for himself a reputation as a forward-thinking risk taker—a leader of the ambitious, imperial-minded faction at the court.

All of this coincided with a moment of rising English expansionism and a mood of national self-confidence that matched Ralegh's own. In the summer of 1588, it was the *Ark Ralegh*—rechristened the *Ark Royal* for the occasion[17]—that led the English navy against the vaunted Spanish Armada. Ralegh had helped design and finance what was widely considered to be the nation's premier war vessel. And although he remained mostly onshore for this campaign as a member of the council of war (he directed defenses for the southwest counties), the stunning English success made his star shine even brighter. He was among the most visible and vigorous of the anti-Spanish coterie within the Elizabethan court, a group that had now successfully defended the kingdom against an increasingly vulnerable Spanish Empire.

If the 1580s represented Ralegh's arrival and smooth triumph at court, the following decade proved far more volatile and bumpy. After the defeat of the Armada came several noteworthy literary endeavors. In 1589, Ralegh introduced at court his friend and fellow poet Edmund Spenser, and the following year Ralegh composed two dedicatory sonnets for Spenser's *Faerie Queene*. He continued to write poetry to the queen, including his most substantial work directed to his cherished mistress, *The Ocean to Cynthia*. He also wrote a spirited tract in support of the *Revenge*, an English vessel lately taken by Spain, in which he vividly described (as he slyly phrased it) the vessel's "heroic" defeat. The same might have been written of Ralegh himself. In early 1592, Elizabeth bestowed on him Sherborne Castle, a country estate in Dorsetshire, and all seemed well. Yet by the summer, Ralegh had suffered an enormous setback when the queen had him thrown in the Tower of London. Why the sudden reversal of fortune? Ralegh had made a daring romantic move by clandestinely marrying one of the queen's ladies-in-waiting, Elizabeth Throckmorton. When a child was born to the couple in the spring of 1592, the incensed recipient of so many of Ralegh's poetic expressions of devotion exploded. Angered by the perceived duplicity of her favorite (and perhaps, too, by the unchasteness of her lady-in-waiting), the queen imprisoned both husband and wife—although the effect was not felt equally by the two. With time, Throckmorton (or Bess, as Ralegh sweetly called his wife) retired quietly to the country, leaving forever the life of the court and its wrenching vicissitudes. Ralegh, meanwhile, upon his release from the Tower, was all but forced to retreat to Sherborne, where he found it difficult to survive without the bracing ups and downs of the court. He bravely persevered, accordingly, in his attempts to win back the queen's favor.

His efforts had both an air of the heroic and a scent of desperation. Ralegh was an innate scrapper: persistent, energetic, ambitious. Yet he also depended on the good graces of others, most particularly Her Majesty, Elizabeth. This awkward dependence is a central theme of Ralegh's career, noted by nearly all contemporaries and expressed here in a striking sporting metaphor:

> Sir Walter Ralegh was one that (it seems) Fortune had picked out of purpose of whom to make an example, or to use as her tennis ball, thereby to show what she could do; for she tossed him up of nothing, and to and fro to greatness, and from thence down to little more than that wherein she found him.[18]

The chronicler makes the point that the great Elizabethan icon, Sir Walter Ralegh, relied for his fame on Fortune, or Lady Luck in our modern phrasing—although one might just as easily substitute another forceful woman, Queen Elizabeth, in this regard. It is equally plausible, however, to describe Ralegh in more proactive terms that highlight his other, more entrepreneuring qualities and his tendency

to force Fortune's hand: to take great risks so that Fortune, who notoriously favors the bold, might intervene on his behalf.

Ralegh's next and certainly most audacious career move was such
a gamble: the decision to sail to Guiana in tropical South America
(present-day Venezuela), with the intent to discover new lands and
riches for the queen and to gain for her the legendary kingdom of El
Dorado. There are at least two remarkable factors that make Ralegh's
adventure stand out, even within the extraordinary annals of Renaissance overseas exploration. First, Ralegh represents one of the rare, if
not unique, cases of a bona fide courtier in America. While many who
journeyed to the New World would later gain stature and elevated status back in the Old, few left the cushy confines of the European court
for the uncharted wilderness of America. Ralegh was a true courtier-
conquistador, and he looms conspicuously in the company of such
lower-standing (and lesser-born) adventurers as Hernán Cortés, Francisco Pizarro, and Diego de Almagro—all of whom became models,
or rather anti-models, for Ralegh (as will be discussed later). Second,
Ralegh narrated his adventure in spectacular and pleasingly accessible
prose, and he promptly published his account. This was exceptional
for a courtier—those of the court generally did not deign to publish,
let alone publicly describe, their intimate thoughts—and unusual, too,
for a conquistador: most conquistadors had their lives and deeds
recorded by later chroniclers or perhaps their secretaries. Although
Ralegh's voyage to Guiana did not generate the piles of gold and silver
amassed in the other great Spanish conquests, or precipitate a lasting
British colonial presence in tropical America, it did produce one of the
most popular travel accounts of the age of exploration and one of the
most successful literary treatments of America to emerge from early
modern Europe. Ralegh was the rare Renaissance hero who could
handle the pen as well as the sword.

Ralegh's valor in America also caught the queen's attention, and, if
he never fully regained his place in her inner circle, he was ultimately
taken back into her court. In this simple sense, the voyage succeeded.
Sir Walter Ralegh thus spent the rest of Elizabeth's reign serving the
queen and campaigning against Spain, albeit in a diminished capacity
and with less stature than before. In 1596, he played a major role in
the raid on the Spanish galleons in the harbor of Cádiz. Although
Ralegh absented himself from the sacking of the town—his leg was
badly wounded in the naval battle, which caused him to limp for the
rest of his life—he gained glory otherwise in his conduct as a soldier
and helped to deliver to the crown a splendid share of the booty. Cádiz

was a national triumph, a turning point in the Anglo-Spanish rivalry and perhaps the equal of 1588. Ralegh next took part in the so-called Islands Voyage of 1597, which brought the anti-Spanish campaign to the Azores, and there was talk of further Atlantic privateering for the queen. Not much progressed on this front, however, as Elizabeth, in the final years of the century and the twilight of her life, retreated more and more from public affairs. A challenge to her power by Ralegh's longtime rival the earl of Essex led to the latter's execution and Ralegh's temporary rise in queenly affection. Yet this moment of grace was short-lived. Elizabeth died on March 24, 1603, and with her went virtually all of the political capital accumulated by her longtime favorite, Sir Walter Ralegh.

"Tanto monta, monta tanto"—as much as the queen takes, she gives even more—it was said of another much-admired Renaissance ruler, Isabel of Castile. The reverse held true, too, and when the last Tudor monarch departed this world, with her went all of the personal favor and royal support that had been granted to her beloved servant. Although Ralegh did stage one final voyage to Guiana, undertaken without the blessing of the new Stuart regime, his political career never fully revived. On the contrary, but for the brief Guiana interlude, he spent the rest of his life in the Tower of London, until his climactic trial and subsequent beheading for treason in 1618.

DISCOVERY, OR HOW TO GET "NEW" WORLDS IN THE RENAISSANCE

Did Ralegh *discover* Guiana? A matter at once seductively simple and delicately intricate, the question of Renaissance "discovery" and Ralegh's place, more particularly, in the annals of British imperial history may come down to a basic word and its multiple meanings. There have been, certainly, some unambiguous answers. Arguing the brief in the affirmative are the numerous scholars over the years who have celebrated Ralegh as the heroic epitome of imperial exploration. The quintessential Elizabethan sea dog, Ralegh has long been heralded precisely for his foundational labors as the "father of American colonization" and credited for his role as the "originating" figure (as one prominent historian has called him) of the British Empire.[19] Others have been more skeptical—such as the Enlightenment philosopher and historian David Hume, who once dismissed Ralegh's claims of discovery "as being full of the grossest and most palpable lies."[20] In

either case, the meaning of words such as *discovery* and *empire* have
so shifted over time that it is difficult to peg exactly what was—and
still is—meant both by critics and boosters. A useful starting point
might be the assertions of the original sources themselves, although
these, too, must be treated with caution. Ralegh's vigorously titled
text, *The Discoverie of the Large, Rich, and Bewtiful Empyre of Guiana*,
is less than fully helpful, since the title was possibly the work of his
London printer (his narrative was not originally planned for publication). A better source may be the text composed by Ralegh's trusty
lieutenant Lawrence Keymis. "I have heere brieflie set downe the
effect of this your second *discoverie*," notes Keymis at the opening of
his report on a second journey to Guiana, "performed and written in
the year 1596."[21] To rephrase the question: What did Keymis mean—
and what would his readers infer—when he described Ralegh's *discoveries* in America?

The great "discoverers" of the Renaissance were generally associated with Spain, and the practice of "discovery" in this period was
widely taken to be a Spanish vocation. (Or it was understood to be
an Italian line of work, since so many of the Spanish-commissioned
voyages were outsourced to Italian navigators such as Columbus,
Vespucci, and Pigafetta.) It certainly appeared by Ralegh's day to be a
field dominated by the protagonists of the Spanish *Conquista* (Conquest), above all the heroic Cortés, the mercurial Pizarro, and the
already controversial Columbus. The near-legendary "discoverer of
the New World," Christopher Columbus never quite comprehended
that his landfalls lay in the Western Hemisphere. To his dying days,
he insisted that he had reached Asia—the Far East, more precisely, in
the vicinity of China—and not America, which was ultimately named
after his Florentine rival, Amerigo Vespucci. Yet Columbus's voyages
established an operational model for, and popular literature of, "discovery" that would shape the terrain for the next century. Discovery in
the Columbian sense was less a matter of exploring or investigating an
unknown space than identifying (if erroneously) and publicizing one's
assertion of primacy. The Admiral of the Ocean Sea, as Columbus
came to be titled, took possession of the West Indies for his royal
majesties by act of proclamation; on this basis, Spain would stake its
claim to the Americas. Less critical than Columbus's navigational feat
or his geographic finds were his public professions of "victory" (as he
phrased it in the opening line of his published letter to Ferdinand and
Isabel) and his habit of stamping his "discoveries" with his personal
mark. This might entail the process of naming islands and ports in

Spanish (often in ways that paid tribute to his royal patrons: Isabella, Fernandina, Juana, and so on),[22] of following intricate Castilian legal traditions (as Cortés most famously did in his foundation of Mexican municipalities), or of describing the landscape he encountered with reference to Spanish touchstones (the weather in Seville or the towers of Granada, for example). Columbus tried to render his finds less exotic than familiar; his discoveries brought "new" worlds—if not necessarily alien or unexplored worlds—under the jurisdiction and cultural control of Spain.

The purpose of this almost feline pattern of marking was to lay claim to a territory for oneself—or rather, for one's patrons. And the larger goal was to help the royal sponsors of the discovery to obtain those advantages that came with the territory. Renaissance discovery, in this sense, less resembles the tradition of Romantic exploration, which ushered nineteenth-century Europeans to the farthest reaches and most exotic locales of the globe, than it does the modern process of identifying new trade venues and making commercial inroads into well-known sources of profit. In the case of the Catholic Monarchs of Spain, who competed so fiercely with their Portuguese rivals, the holy grail of discovery was a new and swifter route to the lucrative spice trade, which had been pursued and speculated upon for years. Vasco da Gama had "discovered" India by successfully rounding the Cape of Good Hope and sailing up the Malabar Coast to reach the port of Goa. With Columbus's journey to the Caribbean, Spain had discovered a new route to the East by sailing west, a fresh commercial opportunity in the Americas, and thus a strategic advantage over its chief European competitors. It gained far more than spices, too. The "discovery" of America also produced for its sponsors—and this applies, as well, to the navigations to India and the Far East—a phenomenal emporium of products: pepper, ginger, and cinnamon (among other coveted condiments) now joined indigo, cochineal, and brazilwood (the latter a source of expensive dyes), silk and cotton (which revolutionized European dress), sugar and tobacco (soon to alter diets and social habits), and a host of other imports that earned immense profits for princes and merchants alike. More broadly, the overseas explorations transformed the lives of Europeans at virtually every level of society. They introduced to Europe new peoples and geographies, exotic flora and fauna, and marvelous artifacts and fabulous tales of the non-European world. (Not lost on some Europeans, however, was the calamitous effect of the so-called discoveries on indigenous populations. See Document 5.) Finally, they generated gold, and this may have been the most salient lesson of discovery. Renaissance Europe marveled above all at the prospect of easy riches—the promise of earthly paradise—and the word *discovery* was perhaps most closely allied in the mind's eye of Ralegh's readers with the glitter of gold.

Discovery, to be sure, consisted of spiritual impulses as well. Queen Isabel of Castile was particularly concerned about the conversion of the natives of America, and she rebuked Columbus when he unloaded a cargo of Indian slaves upon his return to Spain. A Christian impulse is otherwise evident throughout the literature of the Spanish Conquista—an enterprise of plainly missionary character, which was in many ways modeled on the Castilian *Reconquista* (Reconquest) of the Islamic-held kingdoms of Iberia. Virtually all of the royal proclamations and edicts, all of the explorers' reports and letters, and all of the published accounts and histories that related to the voyages of discovery make prominent mention of godly duty, divine guidance, and religious intentions. This goes for Portuguese voyages to the East Indies as well. Yet intentions, naturally, can differ from outcomes, and the results of the Renaissance voyages of discovery suggest that worldly motives commonly trumped spiritual ones. The often frank admissions of many of the discoverers themselves also belie the strength of their religious priorities. Bernal Díaz del Castillo, a Spanish soldier who left a firsthand account of the conquest of Mexico, offered a contradictory assessment of his aspirations when he pronounced his desire "to serve God and his Majesty, to give light to those in darkness, and to grow rich." Cortés himself was unequivocal and characteristically blunt when he declared his objective upon setting out to conquer Mexico: "to win gold, not to plow fields like a peasant or priest." Cortés's "discovery" of New Spain—a harsh, swift conquest that reaped stunning, ungodly riches—presented an archetype for others to contemplate. (See Document 8.) It clarified the temporal, rather than the spiritual, nature of the action taking place in America. The humanist chronicler Peter Martyr summed up the situation well in his early-sixteenth-century history of the Conquista: "It is in reality the thirst for gold no less than the covetousness of new countries," he observed dryly, "which prompted the Spaniards to court such dangers." Martyr had in mind the first generation of discoverers, yet the case of Pizarro, another rough-hewn warrior turned discoverer whose exploits followed shortly after those of Cortés, confirmed this image and another of Martyr's sage judgments: "It is a common thing to observe amongst men that arrogance accompanies success"—a conquistador truism if there ever was one.[23]

Fortune favors the bold, noted Cortés and many of his conquistador cohort, echoing their contemporary, Niccolò Machiavelli, who cited the classical adage in *The Prince.* Conquest and discovery, as a Spanish vocation, implied boldness and audacity. Lawrence Keymis referred explicitly to this formula in his appeal to English readers. "The profit then by their example to be gathered," he wrote apropos of the triumphs of the Spanish conquistadors, "is not to loose [sic] opportunity by delay or to seeme fearfull and dismayed, where there is no cause of doubt." "We cannot denie," he added, "that the chiefe commendation of vertue doth consist in action."[24] Yet Keymis otherwise offered a stinging criticism of the Spanish project in America, particularly Guiana, which had been scarred by the unremitting brutality and rapacity of Spain. (See Las Casas's catalog of "tyrannies" in Document 5.) Keymis's language in this passage and others suggests a countermodel of conquest: one that combined the much-heralded quality of "action" with the equally laudable quality of "virtue." Indeed, this was the self-declared contribution of England to early modern discovery. Whereas Spain had shown the way to American riches, England, by sharp contrast—note Keymis's assertive double negative, "cannot denie"—would demonstrate the path to "virtue" in the New World. And the vanguard of English discovery? In his *Relation of the Second Voyage to Guiana* (1596), Keymis held up as the avatar of virtue in America his erstwhile patron and mentor. When it came to discovery, Sir Walter Ralegh was the anti-Spaniard.

Ralegh embodied early English aspirations in America, his case offering the epitome of the Anglo-American mission of the late sixteenth century. In contrast to the cruel if vigorous Conquista practiced by the Castilians, Ralegh represented his actions (and encouraged others to represent them, too) as part of what might be called a "courteous conquest." He would surpass Cortés, he averred, in terms of bravery and force of arms, yet all the while comport himself with "virtue" and "civility" (to use two favorite Elizabethan terms) toward the otherwise put-upon Indians. As such, Ralegh became the signal figure in Elizabethan England's challenge to Habsburg Spain. Meanwhile, he provided Europe with an alternative vision of American discovery. None of this implies, it should be stressed, that Ralegh and the English turned up their noses at the prospect of easy wealth and a rich harvest of American gold; far from it. They intended, however, to have their gold *and* their gilded reputations by becoming the most worthy performers on the imperial stage. Here Ralegh followed a distinctly English tradition. Sir Thomas More had first tackled the topic of moral, or virtuous, imperialism in his early-sixteenth-century masterpiece *Utopia* (1516). More depicts the Utopians as an island nation of upstanding citizens and sometime colonialists. Their overseas initiatives are understood, in part, as a means of conveying "civility" to those societies less blessed by the habits of Christian humanism. And although More was clearly commenting on, and indeed criticizing, his own society, he placed the Utopians and the recipients of their colonial largesse in the West. An early allusion to Vespucci all but confirms that More's colonial musings—his inquiry into so-called civility—had been prompted in part by the voyages of American discovery.[25] Closer to Ralegh's day were the imperial strategies espoused by Richard Hakluyt, compiler of the great "epic" of British expansion, *The Principall Navigations, Voyages, and Discoveries of the English Nation* (1589). Hakluyt used his translation of Hernando de Soto's voyages as an occasion to contemplate for his readers a "benign" policy toward the Indians: "To handle them gently, while gentle courses may be found to serve, it will be without comparison the best."[26] "Without comparison" refers to competing colonial programs, which Hakluyt deemed unacceptable for the English nation. The same sentiment can be found in the prose of Hakluyt's patron, Sir Walter Ralegh, who made a career precisely of competing with Spain and trying to best them at their own game. More broadly, much of the thrust of English discovery by the final decades of the sixteenth century was to escape the shadow of Spain and to demonstrate an alternative paradigm of Renaissance discovery.

These late-sixteenth-century stirrings do not mark the commencement of English efforts in America. England's forays into the New World were notoriously "belated," "tardy," and "spasmodic," as scholars have long pointed out; but they might more aptly be described as simply ineffectual.[27] For voyages were made and initiatives taken in the century before Ralegh, yet with little lasting achievement. The early expeditions (1497–1498 and 1508–1509) of the Cabots, father and son—a Genoese family in the service of Henry VII—failed to produce even a toehold in America, and more than half a century would pass before further energies were expended on voyages abroad. The failure was, in part, the crown's, since both Henry VII and Henry VIII showed scant interest in overseas projects while preoccupied with religious and political problems at home. This contrasts with the alacrity with which the Spanish kings, Charles V and Philip II, pursued a New World empire, a process that *followed* religious and political consolidation. English inaction also derived from the relative indifference of the merchant class, which spent the first half of the century bolstering its share of the Continental cloth trade. This commerce collapsed, however, by mid-century, giving the English greater incentive to seek profits elsewhere. Still, little of note was achieved through the first decades of Elizabeth's reign, and certainly few lasting profits were made.[28]

Those Elizabethans who finally did venture westward tended to pursue two paths of "discovery." The more dramatic cases of Sir John Hawkins and Sir Francis Drake, the legendary English "pirates" who preyed on Spanish shipping (with the queen's tacit permission) in the 1560s and 1570s, constituted something akin to a hit-and-run strategy. The goal was quick and low-cost profits rather than sustained and hard-won settlement, and no colonization as such (and relatively few lasting profits) resulted from their actions.[29] Another tact, originally advanced in the chambers of geographers, revived the age-old dream of finding a new route to the Indies. English theorists and navigators, however, in contrast to their Spanish and Italian colleagues, speculated on finding a *northerly* path to Cathay (as China was known) by sailing above the newfound hemisphere. The pursuit of the fabled Northwest Passage enticed English (and later American) voyagers well into the nineteenth century—as late as Thomas Jefferson, who in 1803 dispatched Lewis and Clark to the Pacific Northwest with this goal in mind. In the 1560s, Sir Humphrey Gilbert pushed a scheme to sail west and then north to reach, by way of the frigid waters cradling Canada, the tropics of Asia. And in the following decade, Sir Martin Frobisher took the lead on a similarly hatched plan, backed by the newly formed Company of Cathay, to navigate the northeastern coast of North America. Frobisher made three expeditions (he entered Hudson Bay in 1576) but earned no real profit, and the company was dissolved. By the time Ralegh entered the scene in the 1580s, the outlook appeared bleak.

Ralegh enjoyed a fairly advantageous view of England's progress toward America. His Devonshire kinsmen had business connections with both Hawkins and Frobisher, and Gilbert was his half brother. The latter had, in fact, engaged Ralegh in some of his plans. When Gilbert received a patent in 1578 to settle Norumbega (as the coastal region between the Hudson River and Newfoundland was then called), he enlisted the young and barely tested Ralegh to command a vessel. Although this expedition fared badly, another voyage was launched five years later, and again Gilbert invited his younger brother to join. This time, however, Ralegh, by now much favored by the queen, remained on land and at court, where he received the chilling news of Gilbert's death in an Atlantic storm. In many ways, this marked the end to the opening chapter of England's history in America. Yet Ralegh was well positioned to pick up the narrative thread—which he promptly did. By the mid-1580s, Ralegh had assumed from Gilbert the mantle of imperial impresario. He adroitly took the lead in England's "western discoveries," pushing his own plans energetically and guiding the efforts of others. The year after Sir Humphrey's death (1584), Ralegh applied for and received a patent from the queen to search out and take possession (in her name) of "remote, heathen, and barbarous lands." He would occupy himself with the Roanoke voyages through the late 1580s and turn to Guiana after that. Through the end of the century—and arguably for the rest of his life—the performance of an American discovery featured centrally in Ralegh's ambitions.[30]

Ralegh's initiatives resembled earlier efforts in important ways, yet they also introduced several vital reorientations of England's overseas enterprise. In April 1584, he dispatched two vessels to reconnoiter the region lying somewhat below Gilbert's latest landfalls; his men ended up surveying the coast off present-day North Carolina, on which they reported enthusiastically. This southerly shift in Ralegh's plan is revealing. Rather than pursuing opportunities in the frigid northern waters, which drew Cabot, Frobisher, and Gilbert, Ralegh set his sights on more temperate lands closer to the heart of Spanish America. He thereby aimed, first, to take the battle more directly to Spain and, second, to settle colonists in a location more promising in the long run. Roanoke Island lies precisely at the latitude of the Strait of Gibraltar—the gateway to the Mediterranean and the traditional Pillars of Hercules, which Spain had adopted from Greek mythology as a symbol of its empire—and it is no accident that Ralegh drew his colonial line to the New World directly from this Old World touchstone. A temperate climate offered the best prospect for agriculture, and warmwater harbors would make possible year-round shipping. "Close" was not quite contiguous, however; Ralegh's plans avoided head-on contact with the Spanish colonies. In fact, he had received by his patent permission to settle only territory unclaimed by other (Christian) nations, and this prohibited a more aggressive policy toward Spain. It did not rule out privateering, though, and in this regard Ralegh's ships followed in the wake of Drake's and Hawkins's.

If the courtier himself did not make the journey, Ralegh participated assiduously in the planning and sponsorship of the Roanoke voyages. Upon the return of the 1584 expedition, he outfitted seven more ships to return and settle the land Ralegh now christened, with exquisite tact, Virginia. His cousin Sir Richard Grenville led the fleet, dropping off some one hundred settlers on Roanoke Island. Here they were expected to survey the land and its resources; make strategic sketches and maps (drawn by the remarkable draftsman John White); conduct research on the natural world and native inhabitants (undertaken by the accomplished mathematician turned naturalist Thomas Harriot; see Document 7); and carry out other preliminary tasks necessary for colonization. Meanwhile, the Lord and Governor of Virginia, as Ralegh now titled himself, drummed up support from investors and promoted the project to his powerful friends at court. He also arranged for Drake to provision the colony the following year (June 1586), yet with things going badly, the settlers asked to be relieved and returned to England. This was done, and when a bewildered Grenville returned shortly after and found no settlers—and failed to get further information from the Indians—he left fifteen men behind to secure the settlement. They were never heard from again. A determined, if disheartened, Ralegh plotted another colonial mission in 1587, this one led by John White and conveying a wider mix of settlers—families and farmers, rather than just soldiers and surveyors—yet it ended worse even than the previous one. After spending the better part of the summer in Virginia (and witnessing the birth of his granddaughter Virginia Dare, the first English child born in America), White returned to England in August to hasten the shipment of supplies. He left eighty-four men, seventeen women, eleven children, and two Indians, who were allied with the English, on the island. What next transpired ranks among the great mysteries of colonial history. Although Ralegh welcomed the encouraging news from Virginia and prepared to outfit a new supply ship, the whirlwind of the Spanish Armada diverted his attentions and energy. By the time White returned to Roanoke a full three summers later, in 1590, the inhabitants had disappeared and the settlement lay in ruins. Despite five years of careful planning, considerable investment, and fierce drive, Fortune had not favored the bold initiatives of Sir Walter Ralegh. He had thus far failed to make his mark on America.

To return, once again, to "discovery": In the opening passages of Ralegh's next American "performance," as the title page of his *Discovery* phrases it, Ralegh establishes a meaning of the term *discovery* that implies a process of learning. He wishes to glean, or discover, from those Spaniards posted in the region a pathway to the Orinoco River. He repeats this sense of the word a few pages later, when he notes that his men had reconnoitered the river a year prior (1594) and that Ralegh now wished "to discover and enter the same" (page 50). Having failed in Virginia, where he had no path to follow, Ralegh set his sights more keenly on the colonial empire of the Habsburgs. He wished, as the text makes clear, to follow in the footsteps of Spain— although he aspired to tread more gracefully and to conquer more productively than had his predecessors. His idea of discovery entailed a recovery of sorts: an improvement on the Spanish model, a re-enactment of the Castilian Conquista, albeit with more admirable and virtuous results. Or, to adopt the theatrical conceits favored by his contemporaries, Ralegh would "discover" a means to outperform his rivals and do so on the central stage of imperial history.

GUIANA, OR EUROPE'S EL DORADO

Guiana is a tropical zone of South America located on the continent's north-central coast, bounded by modern Venezuela to the north and Brazil to the south and west (see the map on page xvi). The region's name derives from an Indian word, *guiana*, or "land of water," and water indubitably encompasses the landscape. Embracing the country to the east and north are the Atlantic Ocean and Caribbean Sea; and grasping into the region's interior, like so many tentacles, are the mighty Amazon and Orinoco rivers, which flow from the highlands through the jungle and down into the ocean. Hovering above this network of circulating liquid are the humid airs and continual rains that nourish and soak the region. Technically, the native term *guiana* refers strictly to the narrow lowlands along the coast and the commonly flooded alluvial plains. But this nomenclature and rather apt assessment of the environment also may apply to early modern Europe's experience of the region more generally, since Old World interlopers tended to restrict themselves to the coast and rivers. They negotiated Guiana by boat.

Over the course of the sixteenth century, Guiana took on a meaning for Europeans at once more precise and more diffuse than the sum of its geographic parts. It loomed large in the minds of many: explorers, utopians, treasure hunters, colonial planners, and, not least, consumers of Renaissance travel literature. For much of its post-Columbian history, Guiana occupied a prime spot in the European imagination as a locus of boundless riches and imperial opportunity; it induced almost mystical (if not mythical) optimism. Guiana was both the origin of paradise and the home of *el dorado*, "the gilded one"—by which was meant the sovereign ruler of an inland empire who had himself ritually covered in the plentiful gold dust of the country. (See Document 3, Figure 8). Whether these unearthly enticements were construed literally or metaphorically, they appealed greatly to Europeans. Columbus himself did much to contribute to this perception. In his third voyage of 1498, he navigated along the coast of Guiana near the mouth of the Orinoco, although he did not actually make landfall on the continent. In what ranks among the most ardent of his New World descriptions, Columbus complained of debilitating exhaustion and sleepless nights, all the while providing an intensely vivid description of what he characterized as the "earthly Paradise": the mountainous expanse of Guiana, identified as the biblical Eden.[31] Vespucci visited the region around 1500 and gave a secular twist to Columbus's quasi-eschatological ruminations by portraying a landscape filled with stunning marvels and great natural wonders. He insisted, too, on the abundance of gold in the flaxen-colored hills beyond the coast— the selfsame site of Columbus's Eden. Vespucci's widely published account, perhaps more than any other early Americana, electrified European readers and established the province that would soon be called Guiana as a byword for paradise—for some quite literally, for others more evocatively.[32] The Spanish conquistadors who would soon descend on the New World felt the strong lure of Guiana and its elusive stores of gold, and they expended great, if mostly vain and obsessive, energy to locate these stores and claim them for themselves.

In *The Discovery of Guiana*, Ralegh describes, in almost scholarly detail, the several prior attempts to unearth Guiana's gold. His goal was to highlight the well-beaten path to the region and underscore the compelling rationale for his own voyage to the tropics. Juan Martínez, a resourceful munitions master from a Spanish exploring party of the first half of the sixteenth century, claimed to have reached the fabulous city of Manoa, the governing seat of El Dorado. Cast off in a canoe after a disastrous gunpowder explosion, Martínez described how he was discovered by local Indians deep up the Caroní (a major tributary of the Orinoco) and led to their capital city. His reports of a gold-plastered emperor, of golden tableware and housewares, and of ubiquitous gold-wrought objects in the courtyards and gardens of Manoa made the rounds among the conquistador class of Castile and ultimately reached English ears as well—as it turns out, by way of Ralegh. The latter received intelligence of Manoa from Don Pedro Sarmiento de Gamboa, whom Ralegh's privateers captured in 1586.

Ralegh also learned from Sarmiento of more recent expeditions in search of El Dorado led by Don Antonio de Berrio. Don Antonio had inherited land in the vicinity of the Orinoco and, upon hearing local legends of mineral wealth, had undertaken a series of missions into the highlands. His tales of infinite riches may have meandered as much as the rivers they described, yet they convinced Ralegh of the valuable prize that awaited a more enterprising explorer. They offered strong evidence, too, of the persistent, and presumably sagacious, efforts of earlier conquistadors to discover the immense prize of Guiana.

Although Spain never succeeded in tapping the rich veins of Guiana's gold, it did send regular expeditions to the region, assert its control over the coastal lands, and, of great tactical importance, station its soldiers on the nearby island of Trinidad. Thus, for altogether different reasons, Guiana took on special meaning to the enemies of Spain—chief among these, Elizabethan England. For those outside the Iberian Peninsula, Guiana appeared as the key to Spanish America, the soft and vulnerable underbelly of this threatening imperial beast. Centrally located between Mexico and the Caribbean to the north, Peru to the west, and Brazil to the south (under Spanish auspices since 1580, when Philip II annexed Portugal), Guiana occupied prime imperial real estate. To obtain this pivotal piece of the Spanish American puzzle was a goal shared by three of Habsburg Spain's arch-antagonists—England, France, and the Netherlands—and Guiana figured, accordingly, in multiple colonial initiatives of the late sixteenth century.[33] The broad and extensive rivers of the area seemed to promise an entrée to the imperial wealth of Spain, leading (as was imagined) directly to the mineral stores of America's interior. Here the strategists anticipated following the Orinoco or Amazon into the jungles in order to gain backdoor access to the silver and gold mines of the mountains—or to reveal an altogether new source of American wealth. Guiana, it was not implausibly posited, could be the next Peru: a "magazine," as Ralegh put it, of superabundant riches. Looking in the other direction, toward the sea, also exposed the advantages of Guiana. Its superior position on the Atlantic and its proximity to the relatively vulnerable islands of the Caribbean suggested a perfect launching ground for privateers: a well-perched nest from which to swoop down on Spanish shipping lanes. Renegade Spaniards had themselves exploited the region for such purposes throughout the sixteenth century, most notorious among them the thuggish Lope de Aguirre. Now the same idea presented itself to the more militantly anti-Spanish factions of northern Europe. To the sea dogs at Elizabeth's court, the rebels of the Netherlands, and the colonial-minded circles of French Huguenots—Protestants all—Guiana was the key to undoing Spain's empire.

Ralegh belonged, directly and indirectly, to these groupings. He counted himself a longtime detractor of Spain and a fierce enemy of the papist church. He had fought for the Protestant cause in France and perhaps alongside Calvinist rebels in the Low Countries. And he had lately earned his bona fides as a privateer, launching raids on the Spanish galleys that ferried the king's booty from America. Now he turned more squarely to Guiana, in which he had more than just a passing interest. The discovery of El Dorado, or at the very least, of an imperial American beachhead for the queen, drove Ralegh's ambitions for much of the 1590s—indeed, for the remainder of his career. It was a veritable obsession around which many of his other concerns revolved, and he spoke about it and apparently dwelled on it regularly. "As for his noble Design in Guiana," John Aubrey noted, "if you happened to speake of Guiana he would be strangely passionate and say 'twas the blessedst countrey under the Sun, etc., reflecting on the spoyling that brave Designe."[34] He corresponded to his patrons about it, too, and nearly one in five of his preserved letters makes mention of Guiana.[35]

Ralegh's reasons for pursuing "his noble Design in Guiana" both overlap with and deviate from the more general interest in the region. They suggest a more particular and idiosyncratic understanding of place and geography. Ralegh certainly comprehended Guiana in generic terms as a region rich in possibilities, yet he also harbored a more personal sense of it as a locus of redemption: Guiana would elevate Ralegh's standing at court at a moment when he most needed a lift. His public expression of purpose is hardly exceptional. Like those who preceded him, Ralegh imagined Guiana's golden hills ("the magazine of all rich metals") just waiting for European miners, and he counted on the voyage to produce a windfall for both the queen and his financial backers (page 47). He went to Guiana to find gold, plain and simple. Having missed the boat, so to speak, to the Aztec and Inca empires, England would now discover for itself, Ralegh proposed, a new realm of prodigious wealth. On a certain level, then, Ralegh recognized in himself—and his readers, of course—a legitimate desire for financial profit, if not quite a sordid instinct for gain. He would become another Pizarro, he ventured, and his supporters so many *"Peruleri"* (Keymis's inventive idiom for those who had been rewarded from America's silver mines), "who, going bare and emptie out of

Spaine, do againe within three or foure years returne from *Peru*, rich and in good estate."[36] Yet while Ralegh might emulate the conquistadors and laud their pecuniary success, he also perceived his voyage in terms antagonistic to Spain. In the wake of 1588, as anti-Habsburg sentiment peaked in England, Ralegh dressed his American enterprise in patriotic garb as a mission to bring the war to the enemy's imperial base. In this regard, he echoed—and received support from—Richard Hakluyt, the leading overseas propagandist of Elizabethan England, who had long advocated a more proactive and extensive engagement with the Habsburgs in order to lay the foundation of (in the words of the great Renaissance magus John Dee) a "Brytish Empire."[37] Hakluyt also promoted colonizing in America, as opposed to merely hitting and running, and celebrated Ralegh as the "Joshua" of Britain's American enterprise. His voyage to Guiana would lead the English to their new American promised land.[38]

Although Ralegh's expedition was defined in such plainly public terms, it also had a personal agenda that would have been equally evident to the attentive reader of the *Discovery*. Ralegh's journey was an act of personal salvation, a "performance," as he repeatedly terms it, for an audience of one: Queen Elizabeth. Consider the chronology of events. After the Roanoke venture, all New World momentum was deflected by the Armada, and Ralegh spent the final years of the 1580s, together with the rest of England, in a defensive mode. In the spring of 1591, he prepared, at the queen's behest, a fleet to resist another anticipated invasion. That September, the *Revenge* was captured by a Spanish squadron, and its commander, Sir Richard Grenville, was killed. Ralegh published a pamphlet to mark the occasion, forcefully defending the loss and celebrating England's heroic challenge to Spain. In January 1592, an appreciative Queen Elizabeth presented Sherborne Castle to her chivalrous "Water," whose star appeared eternally ascendant. Yet it was not. As Ralegh was preparing, composing, and organizing, as befit a rising courtier and royal favorite, he also was anticipating a child, finally born in March 1592. At once, Ralegh and his wife, Bess, felt the queen's wrath. They fell vertiginously out of favor—the queen would not even consent to see them—and landed in the Tower of London by early summer. Although Elizabeth authorized Ralegh's temporary release in September to supervise the unloading of a captured Portuguese ship (Ralegh was the only one deemed able to quiet the mob), it took until the winter for her to show sustained mercy. Bess and Walter were sent home at Christmas but banished indefinitely from the court. A gallant in disgrace, Ralegh left London for the country. He was now in exile. In this predicament, he undertook what he imagined would be a daring "discovery" in America, a feat that would generate a substantial prize. Guiana was intended as a dramatic gesture for the queen; it was Ralegh's ticket back to court.

Seen in this light, Guiana took on a distinctive meaning for Ralegh. It served as an extension of the court, a stage on which to perform knightly actions and seek redemption from the queen. It was a most remarkable stage at that. Although high-ranking Renaissance gentlemen may have moved from one court to another and perhaps traveled on diplomatic missions, they rarely ventured across oceans and up uncharted rivers. In the powerful circles of London and at the court itself, Ralegh's action raised eyebrows. An arduous transatlantic sailing, a risky reconnaissance of the tropics, several months aboard a ship with soldierly rabble—all of this posed genuine risk. As a rule, Elizabethan courtiers stayed away from jungles. None of Ralegh's courtly peers would have contemplated such a journey (Drake, Gilbert, and Grenville hardly enjoyed the royal access or status of Ralegh), and in the end, some doubted that he had made the voyage at all. Many of Ralegh's enemies accused him of hiding out in Land's End, on the west coast of England, and feigning the whole ordeal. It was simply inconceivable that he had done such a thing. One commentator, writing in the mid-twentieth century, considered Ralegh's Guiana adventure "in the slang of today an 'advertising stunt'"—an anachronism, to be sure, yet one that gets at the performative aspect of the gesture.[39] It was certainly exceptional and a testament both to the fecklessness (some might say desperation) of the fallen courtier and the lure of the New World. The voyage ultimately bespeaks push as well as pull: the demand Ralegh felt to regain royal favor (having been shoved out of court) and the lure Guiana exercised on the Renaissance imagination.

And this suggests a final purpose of the voyage: curiosity. Ralegh had a genuine interest in the world, including the world outside the court, and he strongly wished to "discover" in that most fabulous of worlds, America. He yearned for the spectacular landscapes and exotic inhabitants, the marvelous beauty and otherworldly richness, so alluringly described by Columbus and his successors. He had, in fact, contemplated an expedition to the East Indies, yet this hardly promised the same wondrous novelty as America.[40] Upon arrival in Guiana, he was not at all disappointed with, and often fully dumbstruck by, the staggering beauty of the tropical world he encountered.

"I never saw a more beautiful country," he gushes in one passage (page 90). "We passed the most beautiful country that ever mine eyes beheld," he reports of the amazing vistas he glimpsed (page 77). Ralegh's astonishment and the almost palpable sense of pleasure he derived from Guiana come across in numerous passages of the *Discovery*, some of which rank among the most lyrical descriptions composed of the New World landscape. They demonstrate a sensitivity to the natural environment that often goes unmentioned in studies of the Conquista. Upon obtaining the upriver country, at the confluence of the Orinoco and Carolí rivers, Ralegh admired a landscape so perfectly lovely that it was "as if [it] had been by all the art and labour in the world so made of purpose." It sheltered marvelous deer that "came down feeding by the water's side, as if they had been used to a keeper's call"; a stupendous variety of fowl and fish "of marvellous bigness"; and, most impressively, the *lagartos*, or alligators, "ugly serpents" that, not improbably, provoked astonishment in Ralegh and his men (page 78).[41]

Along with the landscape and *lagartos*, Ralegh marveled at the indigenous peoples of Guiana, with whom the English courtier professed to have a special rapport. To follow the complex trail of native groups and caciques (chiefs) who make an appearance in Ralegh's text is a daunting task. The Indian names listed in the *Discovery* do not readily agree with those of modern ethnography. And although Ralegh has been lately rehabilitated as a fairly able ethnographer—his observations on native society and tribal polity have been given greater credence in recent scholarly literature—there remains much in his description that is less than precise, not least his habit of conflating the many indigenous peoples he contends with into the catchall category "Indians." These would have included the Iaos, Tivitivas, Ciawani, Warao, Waraweete, Orenoqueponi, Sayma, Wikiri, Aroras, Assawai, Nepoyos, Arwacas, and more. Ralegh did understand a broad division, long accepted by Spanish explorers, between *aruacas* and *caribes*, two adversarial "tribes" (comprising, in fact, numerous indigenous groups that may have been related linguistically), one meant to be "gentle" and accommodating (the Arawaks, or Taino as they are called in the Caribbean), the other "savage" and cannibalistic (hence "cannibal," derived from "Carib"). Quite often, the "gentle" Indians included those coastal groups that had been subdued and assimilated—"civilized," by European standards—while "savage" denoted those groups inhabiting the interior that had fiercely resisted European incursions and, not unrelated, were deemed beyond "civility." Ralegh claimed to have forged a special friendship with the natives he met (*aruacas*) and proposed that the "Guianians" would eagerly ally with the English against their mutual Spanish enemy.[42] When Ralegh showed an assembly of native leaders a picture of the queen—an image he apparently traveled with—"which they so admired and honoured," Ralegh observed, "as it had been easy to have brought them idolatrous thereof" (page 50). Along with the Indians he met, Ralegh provides a roster of those not quite encountered—"wondrous" races sometimes described with skepticism, other times with nary a word of doubt. A tribe of women warriors known as Amazons; a nation of men "whose heads appear not above their shoulders" called Ewaipanoma, or Acephali (headless men), to use the term from ancient Greek mythology that doubtlessly shaped Ralegh's descriptions (page 92; see also Document 3, Figure 6); wily philosopher-caciques who lived beyond a hundred years; varied races of flesh-eating cannibals: Guiana was truly a magazine of marvels. Things seen no less than imagined, in brief, would have recommended the country of Guiana to the inquisitive and intrepid knight, Sir Walter Ralegh.

To summarize: Ralegh ventured to the New World and risked the jungles of Guiana for several reasons. First, he wished to discover the way to El Dorado and unearth the lodes of gold that reputedly filled its hilly interior. Second, he launched his voyage as a preemptive strike against Habsburg Spain, insofar as Guiana well fit English geopolitical strategy of the late sixteenth century. Third, actions in the New World induced reactions in the Old World, and Ralegh intended, with his rather exceptional feats of courage and heroism, to win hearts and regain standing in the court of royal opinion. Finally, Ralegh's voyage to Guiana reflects the strong inclination of a quintessential "Renaissance man" to explore and discover. His agenda as a courtier notwithstanding, Ralegh had a lively curiosity in overseas worlds, and America represented the most intriguing and enticing world of his day. Ralegh's Guiana strategy was an extraordinary gambit undertaken under extraordinary circumstances. A disgraced courtier at a critical crossroads in England's imperial history, Ralegh thus embarked on a journey to the tropical heart of America.

RALEGH'S *DISCOVERY OF GUIANA,* OR TEXT IN CONTEXT

Ralegh set sail for Guiana on February 6, 1595. The year before, his longtime partner in privateering, Captain Jacob Whiddon, had led a reconnaissance mission to the region. This time, however, the "Shepard of the Ocean," as Edmund Spenser famously called his seafaring friend, took the helm himself.⁴³ Ralegh led a squadron of four ships along the western coast of Africa and across the Atlantic to the Caribbean, veering south to the island of Trinidad, where he weighed anchor on March 22. After refreshing his men, he quickly dispersed the Spanish garrison and took their commander, Don Antonio de Berrio, prisoner. From Don Antonio, Ralegh extracted critical intelligence pertaining to the lay of the land and the history of the *doradistas* who had preceded him: those conquistadors who had endeavored earlier *entradas* into the tropical interior of Guiana in search of El Dorado. Suitably informed, Ralegh proceeded inland. He rigged a makeshift galley, designed to navigate the low-lying delta that guarded the river, and outfitted it with sixty men. Four smaller vessels carried another forty men into the hot, humid, and frequently drenched maze of waterways and tributaries that wended their way into the Orinoco. The seagoing ships were moored in the harbor off Trinidad, where they would wait for the explorers to return—presumably bearing cargoes of gold.

Although sightings of gold did occur, these failed to generate the cargoes and profits imagined. In truth, the expedition did not fare terribly well. From the outset, morale was low, a problem that only compounded with time. Above all, the heat took its toll. The mostly West Countrymen who joined Ralegh on his jungle mission could barely abide the humidity of the tropics (Guiana lies some 10° latitude from the equator), and the farther they ventured into the interior, the more sweltering and oppressive conditions became. The current also opposed them, flowing increasingly against the English boats as they made their way up the delta. To make matters worse, rations soon began to run low. The tantalizing prospect of locating precious metals and encountering the famed city of Manoa and its gilded monarch certainly encouraged Ralegh to persevere and gave him grounds to goad his men on. Ralegh also was keen to pursue "diplomacy" with the inhabitants of the region; time and again, he proclaimed how imperative native alliances would be for his anti-Spanish project. (This did not preclude, however, his "determination" "to hang the [Indian] pilot" of his boat, who was falsely suspected of leading the expedition into a Spanish ambush.) And Ralegh made much of the exotic flora and fauna he witnessed. The pineapple he ate was "the princess of fruits," and the armadillo he glimpsed was likened to a rhinoceros. Along with these natural specimens, Ralegh collected fabulous anecdotes: of fierce women warriors, headless savages, and the tropical "paradise" believed to lie just around the bend. Upon reaching the Caroní River in early June, Ralegh encountered the most glorious countryside he claims ever to have seen, a landscape of unmatched natural beauty and indubitable mineral wealth. They had reached the threshold of Manoa, he believed. Yet they had also reached the end of their provisions, energy, and time. With the rainy season nearly upon him, Ralegh chose to forgo "present profit" for anticipated future gain, and he turned his flotilla around—though not without collecting a few gold-colored specimens from the rocks along the riverbanks. With the current now flowing in his favor, Ralegh headed downstream in late June. In Trinidad, he found his ships unharmed, and following one final (and fruitless) round of raids in the Spanish Main (the northern coast of South America), the expedition set sail for England. Ralegh reached Cornwall in September 1595, bearing only gold-colored stones of questionable value.

In the annals of overseas exploration, Ralegh's Guiana voyage can hardly be deemed a success: he did not reap any profit for his backers and failed to overthrow Spain in America. Yet if his journey fared less than spectacularly, the same cannot be said of his treatment of the affair in textual form. For the public version of the voyage had a sensational effect; *The Discovery of Guiana* was utterly successful. Ralegh's account of his expedition was published almost at once upon his return, translated thereafter into several languages, and soon circulated throughout Europe in multiple printed forms and editions. And with good reason. Ralegh's brisk prose presented readers with a superb adventure story—an intrepid English knight's explorations among the wild rivers and Indian tribes of tropical America—while also offering an imperial call to arms for those who would challenge Spain's hegemony in America. It electrified audiences not only in England but also on the Continent, where it rapidly became one of the bestsellers of the age of discovery. Indeed, a distinction can be drawn between the original manuscript, quickly composed and rushed to press, and the various printed editions that derived from it. Ralegh, in fact, worked under a somewhat peculiar deadline. Upon his return, detractors quickly cast doubt on the voyage, especially its protagonist's claims of making "discoveries" and locating gold in America. Some expressed the suspicion that the alleged hero had never even left Cornwall. To counter such scurrilous talk, Ralegh hastily drafted a description of the journey (or completed a draft already begun aboard the ship), which he intended to circulate in manuscript among opinion makers at the court. Yet a month or so later, he shifted gears and made the critical, and in many ways innovative, decision to pursue a more ambitious plan: to publish his news of the "large, rich, and beautiful empire of Guiana" and launch his narrative on the court of public opinion. Thus inspired, Ralegh completed the text of the *Discovery* in a matter of weeks and soon delivered it to a London printer.[44] And once out of his hands, the published account took on a life of its own. Editions in Latin, German, and Dutch, printed in large and small formats and commonly including illustrations, maps, and other graphic materials, soon communicated Ralegh's story to the widest possible audience.

Ralegh's *Discovery* justly earned its popularity; it is a work of admirably broad appeal. It is also a work of exceptional qualities, which sets it apart from contemporary volumes of Americana in more ways than one. To begin with, its author enjoyed a relatively high status for this sort of fare, a fact that was doubly distinctive. Courtiers rarely partook of dangerous overseas voyages, and they infrequently published books. Elizabethans of high station did their best precisely to steer clear of the grubby world of print; they avoided the "stigma of print," preferring instead to circulate their prose (and poetry) in the more exclusive medium of manuscript. Ralegh stepped out of this aristocratic pattern not only by journeying to the tropics but also by bypassing the courtly mode of expression and taking his case directly to the people. Ralegh's status made his publication something of a rarity within the genre of exploration literature.[45] That genre was itself distinctive. America presented Europeans not only with a new world but also with a new topic for European prose and poetry. It offered fresh opportunities for literary innovation. Travel literature had flourished, of course, well before 1492, and there were several medieval and ancient traditions of geographical writing. Yet these literary conventions did not fully correlate with the prospect of a *new* world and with the novel challenges of writing at once about exploration and discovery, unidentified nature and unclassified ethnography, imperial history and colonial rivalry, and much more.

For all these reasons, America encouraged literary experimentation, and Ralegh made the most of this opportunity. From a generic perspective, *The Discovery of Guiana* is a remarkably innovative and capacious work; it encompasses several literary forms and rhetorical strategies, all neatly packaged in a single volume. Ralegh composed a prose narrative — a form of writing that, if taken for granted in modern literature (that is, nonfiction), did not enjoy such widespread currency before the late sixteenth century — and his text encompasses disparate forms of prose.[46] The *Discovery* opens with a large section of history (relating the prior exploration and colonization of Guiana by the Spanish); reverts next to geography (a prose tour of the natural resources and exotic landscapes that Ralegh traversed); and includes along the way plenty of passages of natural history and ethnography (descriptions of the flora and fauna of the tropics and observations of the local Indian groups). The volume also comprises a standard travel narrative, which logs the salient details of Ralegh's mostly naval voyage; and at times it veers toward the more fabulous terrain of travel literature—the frankly fictional form of prose that was most common in medieval travel writing. Throughout, too, Ralegh includes portions of court-directed rhetoric that might come under the rubric of political discourse—public relations, as it were, which commonly appeared in early modern pamphlet literature—and he pauses at several junctures in the narrative to offer effusive praise for the queen, or royal encomium. It would be hard to categorize the work in its entirety, since it encompasses so many different forms, or genres.[47] It might be easier and more productive simply to conclude that Ralegh created a wholly new vehicle for travel literature, which would serve for years to come as the foundation of a brand of travel writing–cum–geography that included measures of imperial posturing and political pleading. Ralegh's work demonstrated, moreover, substantial rhetorical sophistication, which set it apart from the more typically wooden prose of contemporary travelogues. A successful publication in its day, the *Discovery* also enjoyed considerable longevity, for its literary eloquence and originality.

If Ralegh experimented with several new ways of writing, he also availed himself of certain older models. This is less evident in a strictly formal sense than from the literary references and rhetorical allusions he makes to traditions of travel writing and patterns of courtly prose. Ralegh was well versed in late medieval travel literature, including the most famous and widely published sample of the genre, *The Travels of Sir John Mandeville* (see Document 4). We know that Ralegh read Mandeville's catalog of wonders from a specific citation in the *Discovery*: Ralegh refers to the authority of "Mandeville" in his discussion of Guiana's Ewaipanoma, that nation of headless men who so occupied the premodern European imagination.[48] Ralegh otherwise alludes to several marvels that likely derived from textual sources, and this suggests his broad familiarity with the fable-filled fare of late medieval travel writing.[49] Ralegh also had models closer to home, which were not directly related to travel and may not leap to mind when contemplating a polemical narrative of tropical exploration. Among the closest literary influences on the great English conquistador was the great Elizabethan poet Edmund Spenser, whom Ralegh befriended in the years leading up to his American adventure. Ralegh likely read a draft of *The Faerie Queene* in 1589, which is around the time Ralegh encouraged Spenser to publish his romantic epic and come to London, where Ralegh would introduce the poet to the queen. Spenser's masterful contribution to English verse, along with his pastoral poem *Colin Clouts Come Home Againe* (1595), are allegorical studies that had much to suggest to Ralegh. *The Faerie Queene* trades in romance and adventure, sylvan marvels and knights-errant; while *Colin Clouts* offers a thinly veiled commentary on life at the Elizabethan court—the very world that the queen's lately fallen servant, Ralegh, sought to reenter by performing epic deeds and "discoveries" in America.[50]

Spenser's epic poetry and Mandeville's fabulous prose shared an allegorical flavor that Ralegh would surely have appreciated. If *The Discovery of Guiana* was an accommodating work, it also included the ingredients of allegory (figurative narrative that conveys a veiled moral meaning). And the rich literary genre of allegory, in turn, helped Ralegh work out the central dilemma of his narrative—and the central objective of his expedition—namely, how to perform a "virtuous" conquest. Like virtually all Renaissance explorers before him, Ralegh inherited his model of New World conquest from Spain. Conquest was *Conquista*, a harshly aggressive manner of seizing possession of lands, inhabited or not, in the name of Castile and Christianity—or at least the assertively Roman Catholic version of that faith practiced by most servants of the Spanish crown. Ralegh acknowledged this model from the outset. He set out to "conquer," he avers in the opening pages of the *Discovery*, and he promises that his feats in the New World will ultimately match those of Cortés and Pizarro. Indeed, he aspires to outdo the Castilian conquistadors: to "perform more than ever was done in *Mexico* by *Cortez*, or in *Peru* by *Pizarro*, whereof the one conquered the empire of *Mutezuma*, the other of *Guascar* and *Atabalipa*" (page 51).[51] Ralegh invokes the legendary Cortés and Pizarro on multiple occasions, simultaneously admiring their military and strategic cunning while denouncing their cruelty and excesses. Cortés especially was perceived as exemplary, the swashbuckling, Machiavellian conqueror of the immense Aztec Empire. The Spaniards' treatment of the Indians, however, provoked the author's most acute rhetorical flashes of censure (see Document

5). Ralegh condemns the appalling violence visited upon the innocent natives of America, who had done the marauding invaders no harm. Spain had "disgraced" a virginal America, a continent that Ralegh configures not only in gendered terms (following classical tradition) but also as a damsel in need of knightly protection. In his famously virile conclusion to the volume—"To conclude, *Guiana* is a country that hath yet her maidenhead, never sacked, turned, nor wrought" (page 109)—Ralegh underscores the quasi-chivalric character of his voyage. He pledges to the Virgin Queen that he has performed, and always will perform, "chastely" and "virtuously" in the New World. He offers himself as a "courteous" conquistador, a worthy knight-errant in the jungles of America.

No small feat: Courteous conquest presents considerable challenges. How can a colonial expedition, with expressly martial and imperial motives, be construed as virtuous and even "gentle"? How can a country peopled by "innocent" and guileless Indians, a land that yet retains its "maidenhead," be justly appropriated for the Virgin Queen and British Empire? How, in short, does one perform a "chaste" conquest? These were the dilemmas that Ralegh needed to sort out in *The Discovery of Guiana*. He did so by resorting to several rhetorical tactics, which generally focus on the *process* of conquest rather than its ultimate goal. To begin with, Ralegh concentrates on contrasts. He highlights the distinctions between the English and Spanish performances in America, emphasizing the rapacity and deceit of the latter and the restraint and honesty of the former. Ralegh thus reassures his readers that the Englishmen under his charge never violated the Guiana women, who were "stark naked," as had their Spanish predecessors. "Nothing," he declares, "got us more love amongst them than this usage" (page 80).[52] Spanish soldiers had otherwise abused the Indians, while Ralegh's men treated them "gently." When English forces slayed the villainous Castilians stationed in Trinidad, Ralegh reports, the natives "much wondered at us" as a result (page 81). Second, Ralegh lets his readers know of the great difficulties and hurdles he had to surmount in America. "Peril, diseases, ill savours, bad fare, and many other mischiefs . . . accompany these voyages," he reports, noting elsewhere that the horrible conditions and deprivations of the ordeal placed him "in a most desperate estate" (pages 91 and 104).[53] Like many knights before him, Ralegh must suffer and endure hardship in his quest for justice: justice for the put-upon Indians, of course, but also just treatment from the English court that had lately spurned him. In the forests of Guiana, Ralegh faced *"opus laboris"* (laborious work), as he dubs it, proving that he must earn his redemption the hard way.

As for the harvest of that arduous labor, Ralegh is more circumspect. The invocation of "laborious work" comes at a pivotal point in the *Discovery* (literally at the midpoint of the book), and Ralegh's word choice and narrative purpose here are revealing. Drifting up the Caroní toward Manoa, the river just beginning to swell with the waters of the oncoming rainy season, Ralegh reports the presence of flaxen-colored stones, which suggested to him and his men the potentially rich veins of mineral wealth buried beneath. Yet "to stay to dig out gold with our nails," he pronounces solemnly, would have been *"opus laboris* but not *ingenii,"* physical drudgery rather than gallant performance. "I could have returned a good quantity of gold ready cast," Sir Walter promises his readers, "if I had not shot at another mark than present profit" (page 80). Ralegh's approach at this critical moment of the narrative—as he draws near to, if only to retreat from, the glittering goal of his mission—might be described as provisional conquest or perhaps heroic failure. His text is filled with numerous such instances of carefully calibrated, earnestly staged disappointments: could haves, would haves, and tantalizing almosts, which never quite yield solid results. Ralegh "could have laid hands on and ransomed many of the kings and cassiqui of the country, and have had a reasonable proportion of gold for their redemption," but he chose "rather to beare the burthen of poverty, then [*sic*] repro[a]ch."[54] He could have gone farther up the river to find El Dorado, even during the wet season, yet refused to drag his men into the hills without better provisions. Quite cannily, Ralegh enlists a rhetorical strategy that permits great feats to be promised, described, and broached, but never convincingly consummated. This allows him to pursue an imperial prize in America without ever committing to the messy business of colonization (let alone the subjugation of Indians); to promise his backers great financial returns without unloading any salable cargoes in London; to boast of heroic deeds undertaken in the New World without finally achieving the rich promises of Conquista. Ralegh, in brief, offers a rhetorical performance without achieving any actions of lasting value—an ironic outcome for this Renaissance man of action.

Ultimately, *The Discovery of Guiana* presents an elusive, "nervous" narrative, as one of its earliest critics put it, which vacillates between the vast potential of the New World and the vast challenges of imperial enterprise. It manages to segue from the immense riches and beauty of America to the noble, if negligible, profits actually yielded by

Ralegh without imparting so much as a mild bout of dizziness.[55] Or, to put this in allegorical terms (as a more recent critic has framed it), the *Discovery* relates a story of "unrequited conquest," with the narrator and chivalric protagonist of the story playing the part of the forlorn lover, as heroic in his effort as in his failure.[56] This permits Ralegh to negotiate the dangerous trial of his narrative: to be a valiant conquistador without actually conquering. The peculiar challenges of the narrative propel a literary style that is simultaneously action driven, while producing no tangible results; oriented to a popular readership, while employing the devices and metaphors of courtly prose; energetic and vigorous in its imperial posturing, while fatalistic in its paradoxical conclusions. "*Guiana* is a country that hath yet her maidenhead," Ralegh submits, yet this tropical paradise could be taken—and thus despoiled—by the overwhelming force of English arms. In the end, and owing in no small measure to this exquisite rhetorical balancing act, *The Discovery of Guiana* "is one of the finest pieces of Elizabethan prose," as yet another admiring commentator has noted.[57] It carries the reader forcefully along, like the mighty Orinoco itself, and thrusts her out to the open sea thrilled and refreshed as much by the journey as by the promised riches passed en route.

EPILOGUE: RALEGH'S LEGACY

We need a word of richer meaning than Fortune to account for the vicissitudes in Ralegh's life.

We have not another such head to be cut off.[58]

Having concluded his discovery in the New World, Ralegh returned to England and London in the autumn of 1595, hoping his performance would win plaudits at court. Largely, it did not, although it did win modest goodwill, if not a full reprieve, from the queen. With time, Ralegh would again alight the stage of court, albeit in a diminished role. Yet he still needed to prove himself, and thus the drama of Ralegh's life carried on. Soon came the Cádiz and Azores adventures (1596–1597), in which Ralegh performed valiantly (and took a cannon shot to the leg), followed by the Essex Revolt, which lifted Ralegh's stock at court at the expense of his longtime nemesis Robert Devereux, second earl of Essex. The Essex drama consumed the court in the final years of Elizabeth's reign, during which time Ralegh partially regained his lost stature. With the queen's death in March 1603, however, all was once again tossed in the air like a "tennis ball," as the popular metaphor of the day phrased it.[59] Under the younger, pacifist, utterly timid, and scarcely anti-Spanish new monarch, James I, all royal favor for Ralegh evaporated. Worse, the new king was distinctly ill disposed toward the older, ostentatiously courageous, vigorous warrior of the anti-Spanish campaigns of the previous sovereign. After a series of miscues by Ralegh and political intrigues by his enemies, Elizabeth's onetime favorite was abruptly arrested and placed in the Tower of London. The putative crime? Ironically—and disastrously for Ralegh—the veteran of 1588 and hero of the Cádiz raids was seized on trumped-up charges of treason and consorting with Spain. In one of the most spectacular trials of its day, and despite widely admired displays of wit and courage on the part of the accused, Ralegh was convicted and summarily sentenced to be hanged, drawn, and quartered—a defining and climactic moment both for the new regime and the old queen's loyal servant.

It did not end there. It has once been said, in reference to Ralegh's poetry, that the author had mastered the "trick of repetition," by which was meant his ability to skillfully revisit themes and even rework lines of verse over the span of his oeuvre, much the way a composer might structure a symphonic work.[60] The same might be said of Ralegh's life more generally, which possessed a natural echo to it. Actions, pursuits, and obsessions all tended to be duplicated and revisited, like so many leitmotifs, producing a discernible rhythm that can be sensed nowhere more clearly than in the final years of his life. Paradoxically, the Ralegh who emerged from the treason trial was a stronger figure than the less-than-popular one who had entered the Great Hall of Winchester Castle. The intemperance of the prosecution and the shabby, prejudicial treatment of this old Elizabethan sea dog won him new admiration from the London crowds. "Never was a man so hated and so popular in so short a time," wrote Sir Dudley Carleton, who esteemed the "temper, wit, learning, courage, and judgment" with which Ralegh conducted himself.[61] At the eleventh hour, James granted mercy. Ralegh would avoid the scaffold for now and enter the Tower for a second tour of duty, this time a life sentence. This prompted a return to several earlier vocations that demanded quiet concentration: scholarship, scientific experimentation, and, of course, literature. Ralegh now performed for a much smaller audience: Thomas Harriot and other men of letters, to be sure, yet also the queen, Anne of Denmark, who eagerly received medical concoctions brewed in Ralegh's lab, and her son, Prince Henry, a happy attendant of Ralegh's informal lectures and musings on the world. The latter topic occupied Ralegh more formally and substantively, too, and this resulted in the monumental *History of the World* (1614), a book that, despite its massive proportions and daunting subject, gained quick popularity and further respect for its imprisoned author.

Along with his return to scholarship and reinvigorated literary production, his new affiliation with doting royals and revived popular esteem, Ralegh also retained his interest in Guiana. It occupied his thoughts, filled his many prison letters, and functioned as "a talisman" in these years, promising to earn him the glory that had eluded him and final redemption.[62] In 1610, 1611, and 1612, Ralegh petitioned the queen and lords (yet, diplomatically, not the king) for permission to voyage anew to Guiana and retrieve the gold that he all but guaranteed would be discovered. He pursued this fervently enough that, in March 1616, permission was finally granted to sail (even if a bona fide royal pardon was not issued) under the condition that Ralegh commit no offense against Spain. Shackled by these barely viable stipulations—only if he were to retrieve adequate gold would his inevitable clash with Spanish troops be forgiven—Ralegh made one final, desperate voyage to the tropics in the spring of 1617. It was an unmitigated disaster. In ill health and obvious pain, accompanied by his son Walter ("Wat") and his old lieutenant Keymis, Ralegh endured a mission that produced one catastrophe after another—and certainly no gold. Poor weather, chronic disobedience, rampant disease, a nearfatal bout with fever that confined him to his ship, a foolish and unsuccessful engagement with Spanish troops, the death of Wat, the suicide of Keymis—the 1617 voyage turned out to be the bleakest chapter of Ralegh's life. It is also the stuff of another book—a book that, tellingly, Ralegh would never write.[63] Upon his return to England, emptyhanded and thoroughly dispirited, Ralegh was arrested, returned to the Tower, hauled before a tribunal (which simply reiterated the charges of 1603), and resentenced to death: yet another echo in his life, although this time with tragic reverberations. Ralegh was led to the scaffold on October 29, 1618, in the morning, as was habit. He spoke, as the chroniclers in the crowd would later record, for the better part of an hour and with great eloquence and calm. He refused the blindfold offered to him, and he even encouraged his executioner— "Strike, man, strike!"—who needed two blows to do the job. "At which time," wrote John Aubrey, based on the numerous eyewitness reports of the event, "such abundance of bloud issued from his veines, that [it] shewed he had stock of nature enough left to have continued him many years in life."[64]

Of course, Ralegh did live on, not least through his *Discovery of Guiana*. Although that book, like many other gestures of Sir Walter's life, appealed expressly to the court and crown, it ultimately gained popularity with a broader reading public in England and beyond. It won high marks as travel and adventure literature, and in the numerous published versions that appeared during the seventeenth century, it became an influential source on the history and geography of tropical America. Multiple editions appeared already in the late sixteenth century, many of them in illustrated or abbreviated form, and this transformed the *Discovery*, furthermore, into one of the most entertaining catalogs of exotic wonders available. Ralegh's text also inspired mapmakers and engravers, who circulated in graphic form his verbal pictures of the headless men, Amazonian women, and ferocious creatures of Guiana. In these miscellaneous, largely pirated editions, which invariably lost some of the polemical edge of Ralegh's original, a fabulous image of America delighted readers. Despite career-long exertions to the contrary, Ralegh had become popular. This was the *Discovery*'s status through the late seventeenth century, and by the eighteenth century, the stern Scottish philosopher David Hume would dismiss Ralegh's influential book as full of lies and denigrate the great Elizabethan conquistador as a charlatan and cheat—and certainly no reliable authority on America.[65]

Hume's morally charged remarks nudge us closer to a final assessment of the character of Sir Walter Ralegh and the overall impact of his American adventures. In the wake of his execution on orders of King James, Ralegh's stock began an ascent that would surge during the Commonwealth regime of the mid-seventeenth century. The staunchly anti-Stuart factions that developed under James and his son Charles I (r. 1625–1649) revered Ralegh as a martyr to the ancient values of Elizabeth's reign. He epitomized the expansive and energetic spirit of 1588, militant anti-Spanish sentiment, and, not least, patriotic Protestantism that seemed to have dissipated under the flaccid leadership of the Stuarts. Ralegh was lionized as a quintessential Elizabethan, a reputation that would only grow with time. By the mid-nineteenth century, Sir Robert Schomburgk, a German-born naturalist-cum-explorer who followed his famous countryman Alexander von Humboldt to the equatorial jungles of America, considered Ralegh a man of great "honor" and ranked his Guiana text among the most valuable reports on the region. Schomburgk, who labored in the tropics for the Royal Geographical Society of Britain, pronounced Ralegh "the father of American colonization and a promoter of commerce and navigation"—and thus "the founder of the British colonial empire."[66] This lofty, proto-imperial reading of Ralegh prevailed for the next century at least. David Beers Quinn also perceived in Ralegh an "originating" figure of the British Empire and credits him with developing a foundational "theory of tropical imperialism."[67] Quinn, it is worth noting, wrote his biographical study, *Ralegh and the British Empire* (1947), at a moment when matters imperial were rapidly dissolving for Britain; and Ralegh's imperial reputation has perhaps faded in recent years along with the standing of empires more generally. More recent studies of Ralegh's efforts in America underscore, ironically, his skills as an ethnographer and even his credentials as a naturalist. There is bona fide gold, it turns out, along the Orinoco.[68] Meanwhile, Ralegh's place as an archetypical Elizabethan seems firmer than ever. He is the supremely capable, multidimensional, vigorously enterprising, unambiguously ambitious, ostentatiously arrogant, and, above all, charismatic player on the stage of early modern history who strived to do so much, even while failing so often. Or, as Ralegh himself put it in his scaffold speech, his "was a course of vanity: I have been a seafaring man, a soldier, and a courtier, and in the temptations of the least of these there is enough to overthrow a good mind and a good man."[69] Whether or not Ralegh was a "good man" lies beyond our judgment, but we might agree that he led an extravagant life that will continue to keep good minds happily busy for years to come.

NOTES

[1]The first quotation, which resembles several other similarly gushing assessments of Ralegh's life, comes from Philip Edwards, *Sir Walter Ralegh* (London: Longmans, Green, 1953), v. The second quotation is from C. A. Patrides, "Ralegh and *The History of the World*," in Sir Walter Ralegh, *The History of the World*, ed. C. A. Patrides (Philadelphia: Temple University Press, 1971), 1.

[2]The story is recounted in Thomas Fuller, *The History of the Worthies of England* (London, 1662), 262; Fuller also comments on Ralegh's "good habit [clothing]" that day. On Ralegh's "sartorial ostentations" (remarked by all court observers, including John Aubrey), see Robert Lacey, *Sir Walter Ralegh* (London: Weidenfeld and Nicolson, 1973), 54, who notes a pair of pearl-bedecked shoes reputed to be worth 6,000 pounds; and Edwards, *Ralegh*, 9.

[3]After years of skepticism, some biographers are now inclined to believe the legend. Walter Oakeshott conjectures that "the mantling of [Ralegh's] crest is a cloak so curiously realistic that it strikes the eye at once as being significant": *The Queen and the Poet* (London: Faber and Faber, 1960), 22–23. Patrides opines that, true or not, "the better part of Ralegh's career is far stranger than fiction": "Ralegh," 2.

[4] Anthony à Wood, *Athenae Oxonienses* (1691), cited in Patrides, "Ralegh," 3, where further references to Ralegh's multiple vocations also are discussed.

[5] David Lloyd, *The Statesmen and Favourites of England since the Reformation* (London, 1665), 487.

[6] See Sir Robert Naunton, *Fragmenta Regalia, or Observations on Queen Elizabeth, Her Times and Favorites* (1641), ed. John S. Cerovski (Washington, D.C.: Folger Shakespeare Library, 1985), 71.

[7] Ralegh's earliest published piece, a commendatory verse for Gascoigne, appears in Gascoigne's *Steele Glas* (1576). He bounced in and out of Sidney's circle but ultimately was more in than out, composing an elegy for Sidney after his death in 1586.

[8] It was Ralegh's life, in fact, that occasioned one of the earliest English usages of the expression "a rolling stone" (which derives from an ancient proverb). His roving efforts in those early years were described by a contemporary as "rather excursions than sieges or settings down, for he stayed not long in a place . . . he was first to roll (through want and disability to subsist other ways) before he could come to repose: and as the stone doth by long lying, gather moss, he first exposed himself to the land service in Ireland," thus avoiding "moss" and gaining a reputation. See William Winstanley, *England's Worthies: Select Lives of the Most Eminent Persons from Constantine the Great, to the Death of Oliver Cromwel [sic] late Protector* (London, 1660), 251.

[9] Naunton, *Fragmenta Regalia*, 72; Lacey, *Ralegh*, 30.

[10] On his library, see Walter Oakeshott, "Sir Walter Ralegh's Library," *Library*, 5th ser., 23 (December 1968): 285–327. On his reading habits, see Benjamin Schmidt, "Reading Ralegh's America: Texts, Books, and Readers in the Early Modern Atlantic World," in *The Atlantic World and Virginia, 1550–1624*, ed. Peter Mancall (Chapel Hill: University of North Carolina Press, 2007), 454–88.

[11] John Aubrey, *Aubrey's Brief Lives*, ed. Oliver Lawson Dick (London: Secker and Warburg, 1949), 254.

[12] Stephen Greenblatt, *Renaissance Self-Fashioning: From More to Shakespeare* (Chicago: University of Chicago Press, 1980). See also Greenblatt's original study of Ralegh, which turned out to be a dry run for his now famous thesis, *Sir Walter Ralegh: The Renaissance Man and His Roles* (New Haven, Conn.: Yale University Press, 1973).

[13] Oakeshott, *Queen and Poet*, 28, citing a letter of 1585 from Thomas Morgan to Mary, Queen of Scots.

[14] Aubrey, *Lives*, 260. For Ralegh's poetic work more generally, see Michael Rudick, ed., *The Poems of Sir Walter Ralegh: A Historical Edition* (Tempe: Arizona Center for Medieval and Renaissance Studies, 1999); and the literary biography of Steven W. May, *Sir Walter Ralegh* (Boston: Twayne, 1989). Literary critics have tended to give Ralegh short shrift as a poet, suggesting that he falls between the cracks; not much regarded as an original poet, he is seen rather as an influence on others. This may result from a reluctance to examine the courtier-poet on his own terms. Ralegh was hardly reluctant to leave evidence of his influence on others (such as Spenser) but more circumspect, as a courtier needed to be, to reveal his own efforts and the influence of others (such as Spenser) on him. The exception to this narrow critical approach is Greenblatt, *Ralegh*, 109–10 and elsewhere; and Rudick's introduction, which notes Ralegh's reluctance to highlight his "author-function" (*Poems*, xix–xxi).

[15] On the Durham House set, see Lacey, *Ralegh*, 110–20. On Ralegh's "science" (an anachronism for this period), see Christopher Hill, "Ralegh—Science, History, and Politics," in *Intellectual Origins of the English Revolution* (Oxford: Oxford University Press, 1965), 131–224. And on his efforts as a historian, see Patrides, "Ralegh."

[16] See David B. Quinn, *Raleigh and the British Empire* (1947; rev. ed., New York: Collier, 1962), 55–56, and note how the Indians' comment offers yet another reference, if from afar, to Ralegh's sartorial distinction.

[17] Upon its name change, the nation's "finest shipping vessel" was bestowed on the queen as well.

[18]Naunton, *Fragmenta Regalia*, 71. A variation of this simile was also recorded earlier in Winstanley, *England's Worthies*, 250–51.

[19]See, above all, Quinn, *Raleigh and the British Empire*, where the protagonist is seen as a foundational figure in the history of the British Empire. V. T. Harlow calls Ralegh "remarkable" and "an epitome"; see Sir Walter Ralegh, *The Discoverie of the Large and Bewtiful Empire of Guiana*, ed. V. T. Harlow (London: Argonaut Press, 1928), xvi. And Robert H. Schomburgk notes Ralegh's "father" role in the history of English expansion; see Sir Walter Ralegh, *The Discovery of the Large, Rich, and Beautiful Empire of Guiana, with a Relation of the Great and Golden City of Manoa*, ed. Robert H. Schomburgk, Hakluyt Society Publications, vol. 3 (London, 1848), xxxiv (hereafter cited as Schomburgk, *Discovery*).

[20]Hume is commonly cited by Ralegh scholars: see, for example, Schomburgk, *Discovery*, xlviii; and Lacey, *Ralegh*, 326, which notes the broader Enlightenment attack on Ralegh's work.

[21]Lawrence Keymis, *A Relation of the Second Voyage to Guiana* (London, 1596), sig. A2r and title page. See also sig. A2v, where Keymis pronounces Ralegh the "Author of these *Discoveries*."

[22]These are the names given by Columbus to Crooked Island, Long Island (in the Bahamas), and Cuba, respectively; see Christopher Columbus, *Select Documents Illustrating the Four Voyages of Columbus*, trans. and ed. Cecil Jane, Hakluyt Society Publications, 2nd ser., 65 and 70 (London, 1930–1933), 1:2. See, more generally, Patricia Seed, *Ceremonies of Possession in Europe's Conquest of the New World, 1492–1640* (Cambridge: Cambridge University Press, 1995).

[23]Pietro Martire d'Anghiera, *De Orbe Novo: The Eight Decades of Peter Martyr d'Anghera*, trans. and ed. Francis Augustus MacNutt, 2 vols. (New York: G. P. Putnam, 1912), 1:193, 214. See also Benjamin Schmidt, *Innocence Abroad: The Dutch Imagination and the New World, 1570–1670* (Cambridge: Cambridge University Press, 2001), 14–30, which places Martyr's text, along with those of Díaz and Cortés, in the context of early encounter literature.

[24]Keymis, *Relation*, sigs. [A4]v–Ar.

[25]More mentions Vespucci in his opening vignette, which takes the form of a fictional conversation between the character "Thomas More" and Peter Giles, an exchange meant to lend an air of realism to the ensuing report; see Thomas More, *Utopia*, rev. ed. (Cambridge: Cambridge University Press, 2002), 10. More also makes the case in *Utopia* for a land-based, "agriculturalist" colonialism in which settlers productively use territory otherwise left idle, an argument that would have had moral (and classical) resonance for his readers; see David Armitage, "Literature and Empire," in *The Origins of Empire: British Overseas Enterprise to the Close of the Seventeenth Century*, ed. Nicolas Canny, Oxford History of the British Empire (Oxford: Oxford University Press, 1998), vol. 1:108. On the humanist imperatives of English colonization, which underscored the "civilizing" mission of the enterprise, see Andrew Fitzmaurice, *Humanism and America: An Intellectual History of English Colonisation, 1500–1625* (Cambridge: Cambridge University Press, 2003).

[26]Cited in Quinn, *Raleigh*, 182. Note, however, that Hakluyt qualifies: "But if gentle polishing will not serve," he continues, "then we shall not want hammerers and rough masons enough" to subdue the native inhabitants of America (ibid., 183).

[27]Nicolas Canny, for example, notes the "relative passivity of the English state in relation to overseas matters"; see "The Origins of Empire," in Canny, *Origins of Empire*, 1–33 (quot. on p. 4). Anthony Pagden simply observes that "the English arrived late in the Atlantic"; see Pagden, "The Struggle for Legitimacy and the Image of Empire in the Atlantic to c. 1700," in ibid., 34–54 (quot. on p. 34). See also Quinn, *Raleigh*, 25.

[28]The exception to this rule—namely, commercial indifference to the Atlantic projects of their competitors—was the Newfoundland fisheries, where English boats joined a swarm of Portuguese, Spanish, and French vessels in pursuit of cod, not gold.

[29]Some of Hawkins's profits came from commerce in slavery, for which he also had the queen's tacit permission; see Harry Kelsey, *Sir John Hawkins: Queen Elizabeth's Slave Trader* (New Haven, Conn.: Yale University Press, 2003); and Harry Kelsey, *Sir Francis Drake: The Queen's Pirate* (New Haven, Conn.: Yale University Press, 1998).

[30]Evidence of Ralegh's abiding interest (the word *obsession* comes to mind) in America comes from his letters; see Agnes Latham and Joyce Youings, eds., *The Letters of Sir Walter Ralegh* (Exeter: University of Exeter Press, 1999), which includes a preponderance of letters that demonstrate a persistent focus on America in general and Guiana in particular. Ralegh's New World patent is quoted in Edwards, *Ralegh*, 10.

[31]Columbus, *Select Documents*, 2:2–47, esp. 34–38.

[32]Amerigo Vespucci, *Letters from a New World: Amerigo Vespucci's Discovery of America*, ed. Luciano Formisano, trans. David Jacobson (New York: Marsilio, 1992).

[33]Richard Hakluyt, for example, was quick to recognize the strategic value of Guiana and propose a "tropical" strategy by which England would target the least fortified portion of Spain's American empire: "All that parte of America eastwarde from Cumana unto the River of Saint Augustine in Bresill . . . there is neither Spaniarde, Portingale nor any Christian man but onely the Caribes, Indians, and salvages. In which places is greate plentie of golde, perle, and precious stones." See Richard Hakluyt, *Discourse of Western Planting*, ed. David B. Quinn and Alison M. Quinn, Hakluyt Society Publications, extra ser., 45 (London, 1993), 51. A similar line of thinking can be found in the Netherlands, where Willem Usselincx, an early proponent of the Dutch West India Company, pushed for a Guiana settlement (and where the writings of Ralegh, not coincidentally, were exceptionally popular); see Schmidt, *Innocence Abroad*, 151, 369.

[34]Aubrey, *Lives*, 257–58. See also Lacey, *Ralegh*, 205.

[35]See Latham and Youings, *Letters*.

[36]Keymis, *Relation*, sig. [A4]v.

[37]See William Sherman, *John Dee: The Politics of Reading and Writing in the English Renaissance* (Amherst: University of Massachusetts Press, 1995), esp. chap. 7; and Armitage, "Literature and Empire," 114.

[38]Hakluyt is cited in Oakeshott, *Queen and Poet*, 31. His allusion to the biblical Joshua refers to the successor to Moses, who led the Israelites into the Promised Land.

[39]Oakeshott, *Queen and Poet*, 31.

[40]The eastern expedition is broached in a letter from Lady Ralegh to Sir Robert Cecil, February 1593, where Bess seeks to enlist Cecil's help in dissuading her husband from any overseas enterprise; see Oakshott, *Queen and Poet*, 61.

[41]Gerald Hammond notes not only the excellent quality of narration in Ralegh's prose but "some marvelous perceptions too—not least of natural phenomena." Hammond offers a good sampling of Ralegh's prose style in Sir Walter Ralegh, *Selected Writings*, ed. Gerald Hammond (Manchester: Carcanet Press, 1984) (quot. on p. 13). Also insightful on matters of style are Greenblatt, *Ralegh*, esp. 110–11 on the passages quoted; and May, *Ralegh*.

[42]See, for example, page 74, which describes the natives of the Orinoco delta—enemies of the "Canibals"—who are "at peace with their [immediate] neighbours, all holding the Spaniards for a common enemy." Numerous passages throughout the text attest to Ralegh's ethnographic interests.

[43]Spenser used this expression to underscore the nautical reputation of his friend and Ralegh's heroics as an Elizabethan "sea dog." See Edward Spenser, "The shepheard of the Ocean by name,/And said he came far from the main-sea deepe": *Colin Clouts Come Home Againe* (1595), lines 66–67. Ralegh would refer to himself simply as "Ocean," as in his verse to Elizabeth, *The Ocean to Cynthia*.

[44]Three separate editions, mildly distinguishable, were printed in early 1596, which gives an indication of the anticipated audience for Ralegh's book.

[45]See Anna R. Beer, *Sir Walter Ralegh and His Readers in the Seventeenth Century: Speaking to the People* (New York: St. Martin's, 1997): "Its [the *Discovery*'s] overtly aris-

tocratic strategies are rejected in favor of other literary modes, the concern with the power of the Queen and her courtiers is displaced by the voices of those who demand a stake in the colonial project" (10). On Ralegh's courtly concern with the "stigma of print," which otherwise did influence his literary (and particularly poetic) production, see Rudick, *Poems*, esp. xviii–xxvii.

[46]Montaigne's *Essais* (1580–1588) pioneered and popularized the form of the essay and helped to usher this genre into England, where it was taken up (if in slightly modified form) by Ralegh's contemporary Sir Francis Bacon (*The Essays*, 1601).

[47]In this regard, it is worth pointing to the "profuseness and variety" of Ralegh's broader literary production, a quality observed by the critic Philip Edwards, who notes the "daunting" challenge that Ralegh's oeuvre presents to readers: *Ralegh*, 127.

[48]See pages 92–93, where Ralegh, though acknowledging that the story of men without heads might be a "fable," doubts that it would be so commonly repeated were it not true.

[49]Ralegh owned most of the key, available works of medieval geography and travel, which are recorded in a list of books he kept in his library at the Tower; see Oakeshott, "Ralegh's Library." For the importance and legacy of John Mandeville (who was the nominal but likely spurious author of a fourteenth-century manuscript on the non-European world), see Iain Macleod Higgins, *Writing East: The "Travels" of Sir John Mandeville* (Philadelphia: University of Pennsylvania Press, 1997).

[50]The web of connections between Spenser and Ralegh, in literature and life, is dense. A bare-bones outline runs as follows: *Colin Clouts* is a poetic narrative of Spenser's entrée to the court, related as pastoral allegory, in which Ralegh fills the role of the "Shepherd of the Ocean," who visits Colin Clouts/Spenser in Ireland and encourages him to journey to London. *The Faerie Queene* contains myriad Raleghana, not least the allusions to Ralegh as represented in the character Timias, a squire of relatively modest origins. Ralegh also composed verse introducing *The Faerie Queene*. Oakeshott sees these affiliations as working toward "a wider purpose: that of assisting in the process of reconciliation between Raleigh and the Queen," whom Ralegh had lately addressed in the *Cynthia* poems from the perspective of the rejected lover; see *Queen and Poet*, 88. More concretely, Oakeshott identifies the Ralegh family copy of *The Faerie Queene* and speculates that Ralegh had it with him on his final voyage to Guiana—a tangible and personal connection between the two men and their lifeworks. See Walter Oakeshott, "Carew Ralegh's Copy of Spenser," *Library*, 5th ser., 26 (1971): 1–21.

[51]Huáscar (Guascar) was the brother of the last Inca emperor, Atahualpa. Note that Ralegh's competitive approach toward Spain was hardly unique. Roger Kuin describes Sir Philip Sidney's Spain complex, in this case regarding Sir Martin Frobisher's navigational feats, which Sidney imagined rivaling those of Magellan: "Querre-Muhau: Sir Philip Sidney and the New World," *Renaissance Quarterly* 51 (1998): 549–85.

[52]Columbus made similar claims of chastity—both his own and, to a lesser extent, his men's—on his first voyage, a point that is discussed in Stephen Greenblatt, *Marvelous Possessions: The Wonder of the New World* (Chicago: University of Chicago Press, 1991).

[53]Many further instances (for example, pages 69 and 75–76) could be cited.

[54]This passage comes from the final (unnumbered) page of Ralegh's "Epistle Dedicatory": Sir Walter Ralegh, *The Discouerie of the Large, Rich, and Bevvtiful Empire of Guiana* (London: Robert Robinson, 1596).

[55]See Schomburgk, *Discovery*, lxiv: "The pure and nervous style in which the *Discoverie of Guiana* is written imparts to it a lasting charm."

[56]Roland Greene, *Unrequited Conquests: Love and Empire in the Colonial Americas* (Chicago: University of Chicago Press, 1999).

[57]Hammond, in Ralegh, *Selected Writings*, 13.

[58]The first assessment comes from Edwards, *Ralegh*, 176. The second, an unattributed cry emitted by one of the many in the crowd who had come to witness Ralegh's

death, is cited widely, including in Raleigh Trevelyan, *Sir Walter Raleigh* (London: Allen Lane, 2002), 552.

[59] See note 18.

[60] Edwards, *Ralegh*, 73.

[61] Cited in Trevelyan, *Raleigh*, 388. Carleton was a trusted court observer and diplomat who would later serve as the English ambassador to Venice.

[62] Ralegh's letters are revealing on this point; see Latham and Youings, *Letters*, especially nos. 192 and following, where Ralegh begins to express his hope to make a second voyage. The "talisman" quotation comes from Edwards, *Ralegh*, 32. See also Aubrey, *Lives*, 258, which notes Ralegh's "passion" for Guiana.

[63] Yet see V. T. Harlow, *Ralegh's Last Voyage* (London: Argonaut Press, 1932), which collects the relevant manuscript material, as well as the posthumously published *Sir Walter Rawleigh His Apologie for His Voyage to Guiana* (1650), which is less a narrative of the voyage than a polemical defense of Ralegh's actions.

[64] Aubrey, *Lives*, 260. Ralegh's final words derive from numerous sources; see, for example, Lacey, *Ralegh*, 382.

[65] See Schomburgk, *Discovery*, xlviii.

[66] Ibid., xxii, x; see also xiv on the "honor" of Sir Walter Ralegh. Note that the venerable Hakluyt Society, founded in 1846 to publish modern editions of the classics of exploration literature, graded *The Discovery of Guiana* highly enough to make it the third volume in its series and selected Schomburgk to edit it.

[67] Quinn, *Raleigh*, 7, 207, and elsewhere.

[68] See Neil L. Whitehead, "The *Discoverie* as Ethnological Text," in Sir Walter Ralegh, *The Discoverie of the Large, Rich and Bewtiful Empyre of Guiana*, ed. Neil L. Whitehead (Manchester: Manchester University Press, 1997), 60–116.

[69] See R. H. Bowers, "Ralegh's Last Speech: The 'Elms' Document," *Reviews of English Studies*, n.s. 2 (July 1951): 215; and Edward Edwards, *The Life of Sir Walter Ralegh* (London: Macmillan, 1868), 1:704.

PART TWO

The Discovery of Guiana

On Thursday, the sixth of February, in the year 1595, we departed *England*, and the Sunday following had sight of the north cape of *Spain*, the wind for the most part continuing prosperous; we passed in sight of the *Burlings* and the Rock,[1] and so onwards for the *Canaries*, and fell with *Fuerteventura* the 17 of the same month, where we spent two or three days, and relieved our companies with some fresh meat. From thence we coasted by the *Grand Canaria*, and so to *Tenerife*, and stayed there for the *Lion's Whelp*, your Lordship's ship, and for Captain *Amys Preston* and the rest. But when after seven or eight days we found them not, we departed and directed our course for *Trinidad*, with mine own ship, and a small bark of Captain *Cross's* only; for we had before lost sight of a small *gallego*[2] on the coast of *Spain*, which came with us from *Plymouth*. We arrived at *Trinidad* the 22 of March, casting anchor at Point *Curiapan*, which the Spaniards call *Punta de Gallo*, which is situate in eight degrees or thereabouts.[3] We abode there four or five days, and in all that time we came not to the speech of any Indian or Spaniard. On the coast we saw a fire, as we sailed

---

[1]Cape Roca, Portugal, the westernmost point of the European continent.
[2]Type of ship commonly associated with Spain (Galicia).
[3]The southwestern extreme of the island, at 10°2′30″ north latitude. Ralegh's reckonings fall consistently two degrees south of the correct locations.

Sir Walter Ralegh, "The Discovery of Guiana," in *Voyages and Travels: Ancient and Modern*, Harvard Classics, 33 (New York: P. F. Collier [1910]), 321–94.

from the Point *Carao* towards *Curiapan*, but for fear of the Spaniards none durst come to speak with us. I myself coasted it in my barge close aboard the shore and landed in every cove, the better to know the island, while the ships kept the channel. From *Curiapan* after a few days we turned up north-east to recover that place which the Spaniards call *Puerto de los Hispañoles*,[4] and the inhabitants *Conquerabia*; and as before (revictualling my barge) I left the ships and kept by the shore, the better to come to speech with some of the inhabitants, and also to understand the rivers, watering places, and ports of the island, which, as it is rudely done, my purpose is to send your Lordship after a few days. From *Curiapan* I came to a port and seat of Indians called *Parico*, where we found a fresh-water river, but saw no people. From thence I rowed to another port, called by the naturals[5] *Piche*, and by the Spaniards *Tierra de Brea*. In the way between both were divers little brooks of fresh water, and one salt river that had store of oysters upon the branches of the trees, and were very salt and well tasted.[6] All their oysters grow upon those boughs and sprays, and not on the ground; the like is commonly seen in the *West Indies*, and elsewhere. This tree is described by *Andrew Thevet*, in his *French Antarctique*,[7] and the form figured in his book as a plant very strange and by *Pliny* in his twelfth book of his *Natural History.* But in this island, as also in *Guiana*, there are very many of them.

At this point, called *Tierra de Brea* or *Piche*, there is that abundance of stone pitch that all the ships of the world may be therewith laden from thence; and we made trial of it in trimming our ships to be most excellent good, and melteth not with the sun as the pitch of *Norway*,[8] and therefore for ships trading the south parts very profitable. From thence we went to the mountain foot called *Annaperima*, and so passing the river *Carone*, on which the Spanish city was seated, we met with our ships at *Puerto de los Hispañoles* or *Conquerabia*.

This island of *Trinidad* hath the form of a sheephook, and is but narrow; the north part is very mountainous; the soil is very excellent, and will bear sugar, ginger, or any other commodity that the *Indies* yield. It hath store of deer, wild porks, fruits, fish, and fowl. It hath

---

[4]Port of Spain, the capital of Trinidad and Tobago.

[5]Indigenous population.

[6]Mangrove oysters, which attach themselves to tree branches and roots during high tide and remain there after the waters recede.

[7]The reference is to André Thevet, the French "royal cosmographer" and author of *Les singularitez de la France antarctique autrement nomée Amerique* (Paris, 1557).

[8]Hard or dry pitch.

also for bread sufficient maize, *cassavi*, and of those roots and fruits which are common everywhere in the *West Indies*. It hath divers beasts, which the *Indies* have not; the Spaniards confessed that they found grains of gold in some of the rivers; but they having a purpose to enter *Guiana* (the magazine[9] of all rich metals) cared not to spend time in the search thereof any further. This island is called by the people thereof *Cairi*, and in it are divers nations. Those about *Parico* are called *Jajo,* those at *Punta de Carao* are of the *Arwacas*, and between *Carao* and *Curiapan* they are called *Salvaios*. Between *Carao* and *Punta de Galera* are the *Nepoios*, and those about the Spanish city term themselves *Carinepagotes.*[10] Of the rest of the nations, and of other ports and rivers, I leave to speak here, being impertinent to my purpose, and mean to describe them as they are situate in the particular plot and description of the island, three parts whereof I coasted with my barge, that I might the better describe it.

Meeting with the ships at *Puerto de los Hispañoles*, we found at the landing place a company of Spaniards who kept a guard at the descent; and they offering a sign of peace, I sent Captain *Whiddon* to speak with them, whom afterwards to my great grief I left buried in the said island after my return from *Guiana*, being a man most honest and valiant. The Spaniards seemed to be desirous to trade with us, and to enter into terms of peace, more for doubt of their own strength than for aught[11] else; and in the end, upon pledge, some of them came aboard. The same evening there stale[12] also aboard us in a small *canoa* two Indians, the one of them being a *cacique* or lord of the people, called *Cantyman*, who had the year before been with Captain *Whiddon*, and was of his acquaintance. By this *Cantyman* we understood what strength the Spaniards had, how far it was to their city, and of *Don Antonio de Berreo*, the governor, who was said to be slain in his second attempt of *Guiana*, but was not.

While we remained at *Puerto de los Hispañoles* some Spaniards came aboard us to buy linen of the company, and such other things as they wanted, and also to view our ships and company, all which I

---

[9]Storehouse or warehouse.

[10]Ralegh uses the term "nation" to refer to both ethnolinguistic and political units—a use that also was common in referring to European peoples of varying linguistic and political organizations (for instance, "Flemish" and "Hollanders"). In this case, he uses "Arwacas" to indicate a native group that had formed an alliance of sorts with Spain, and "Jajo" (Yao) to designate a group that had a distinct, pre-Spanish ethnic identity.

[11]Anything.

[12]Stole: came secretly or stealthily.

entertained kindly and feasted after our manner. By means whereof I learned of one and another as much of the estate of *Guiana* as I could, or as they knew; for those poor soldiers, having been many years without wine, a few draughts made them merry, in which mood they vaunted[13] of *Guiana* and the riches thereof, and all what they knew of the ways and passages; myself seeming to purpose nothing less than the entrance or discovery thereof, but bred in them an opinion that I was bound only for the relief of those English which I had planted in *Virginia*, whereof the bruit[14] was come among them; which I had performed in my return, if extremity of weather had not forced me from the said coast.

I found occasions of staying in this place for two causes. The one was to be revenged of *Berreo*, who the year before, 1594, had betrayed eight of Captain *Whiddon's* men, and took them while he departed from them to seek the *Edward Bonaventure*, which arrived at *Trinidad* the day before from the *East Indies*: in whose absence *Berreo* sent a *canoa* aboard the pinnace only with Indians and dogs inviting the company to go with them into the woods to kill a deer. Who, like wise men, in the absence of their captain followed the *Indians*, but were no sooner one arquebus[15] shot from the shore, but *Berreo's* soldiers lying in ambush had them all, notwithstanding that he had given his word to Captain *Whiddon* that they should take water and wood safely. The other cause of my stay was, for that by discourse with the Spaniards I daily learned more and more of *Guiana*, of the rivers and passages, and of the enterprise of *Berreo*, by what means or fault he failed, and how he meant to prosecute the same.

While we thus spent the time I was assured by another *cacique* of the north side of the island, that *Berreo* had sent to *Margarita* and to *Cumana* for soldiers, meaning to have given me a *cassado*[16] at parting, if it had been possible. For although he had given order through all the island that no Indian should come aboard to trade with me upon pain of hanging and quartering (having executed two of them for the same, which I afterwards found), yet every night there came some with most lamentable complaints of his cruelty: how he had divided the island and given to every soldier a part; that he made the ancient *caciques*, which were lords of the country, to be their slaves; that he

---

[13]Bragged.
[14]Report or rumor.
[15]Harquebus: a portable firearm of varying size.
[16]*Cachado*: a blow.

kept them in chains, and dropped their naked bodies with burning bacon, and such other torments, which I found afterwards to be true. For in the city, after I entered the same, there were five of the lords or little kings (which they call *caciques* in the *West Indies*) in one chain, almost dead of famine, and wasted with torments. These are called in their own language *acarewana*, and now of late since English, French, and Spanish are come among them, they call themselves *captains*, because they perceive that the chiefest of every ship is called by that name. Those five *captains* in the chain were called *Wannawanare*, *Carroaori*, *Maquarima*, *Tarroopanama*, and *Aterima*. So as both to be revenged of the former wrong, as also considering that to enter *Guiana* by small boats, to depart 400 or 500 miles from my ships, and to leave a garrison in my back interested in the same enterprise, who also daily expected supplies out of *Spain*, I should have savoured very much of the ass;[17] and therefore taking a time of most advantage, I set upon the *Corps du garde* in the evening, and having put them to the sword, sent Captain *Caulfield* onwards with sixty soldiers, and myself followed with forty more, and so took their new city, which they called *St. Joseph*,[18] by break of day. They abode not any fight after a few shot, and all being dismissed, but only *Berreo* and his companion, I brought them with me aboard, and at the instance of the Indians I set their new city of *St. Joseph* on fire. The same day arrived Captain *George Gifford* with your lordship's ship, and Captain *Keymis*, whom I lost on the coast of *Spain*, with the *gallego*, and in them divers gentlemen and others, which to our little army was a great comfort and supply.

We then hastened away towards our purposed discovery, and first I called all the captains of the island together that were enemies to the Spaniards; for there were some which *Berreo* had brought out of other countries, and planted there to eat out and waste those that were natural of the place. And by my Indian interpreter, which I carried out of *England*, I made them understand that I was the servant of a queen who was the great *cacique* of the north, and a virgin, and had more *caciqui* under her than there were trees in their island; that she was an enemy to the *Castellani*[19] in respect of their tyranny and oppression, and that

---

[17]The implication is that, for the reasons outlined, Ralegh preferred to act aggressively (as a lion might attack an ass).

[18]The original San José de Oruña, founded by Berrio in 1592.

[19]Castilians: the Spanish. A variation of this name, Castilanos, persisted among the Indians of the upper Orinoco River into the mid-nineteenth century.

she delivered all such nations about her, as were by them oppressed; and having freed all the coast of the northern world from their servitude, had sent me to free them also, and withal to defend the country of *Guiana* from their invasion and conquest. I shewed them her Majesty's picture, which they so admired and honoured, as it had been easy to have brought them idolatrous thereof. The like and a more large discourse I made to the rest of the nations, both in my passing to *Guiana* and to those of the borders, so as in that part of the world her Majesty is very famous and admirable; whom they now call EZRABETA CASSIPUNA AQUEREWANA, which is as much as Elizabeth, the Great Princess, or Greatest Commander. This done, we left *Puerto de los Hispañoles*, and returned to *Curiapan*, and having *Berreo* my prisoner, I gathered from him as much of *Guiana* as he knew. This *Berreo* is a gentleman well descended, and had long served the Spanish king in *Milan, Naples*, the *Low Countries*, and elsewhere, very valiant and liberal, and a gentleman of great assuredness, and of a great heart. I used[20] him according to his estate and worth in all things I could, according to the small means I had.

I sent Captain *Whiddon* the year before to get what knowledge he could of *Guiana*, and the end of my journey at this time was to discover and enter the same. But my intelligence was far from truth, for the country is situate about 600 English miles further from the sea than I was made believe it had been. Which afterwards understanding to be true by *Berreo*, I kept it from the knowledge of my company, who else would never have been brought to attempt the same. Of which 600 miles I passed 400, leaving my ships so far from me at anchor in the sea, which was more of desire to perform that discovery than of reason, especially having such poor and weak vessels to transport ourselves in.[21] For in the bottom of an old *gallego* which I caused to be fashioned like a galley, and in one barge, two wherries,[22] and a ship's boat[23] of the *Lion's Whelp*, we carried 100 persons and their victuals for a month in the same, being all driven to lie in the rain and

[20]Treated.

[21]Ralegh engages here in a typical conquistador ploy: rhetorical exaggeration (which cannot be verified by European readers). The farthest point reached by Ralegh—the mouth of Caroní River—is about 100 miles from Trinidad. Taking into account the winding river and delta passages, he and his men might have traveled some 250 miles, but nothing approaching the 400 claimed. The 600-mile estimate Ralegh proposes would place Guiana on the upper Caroní (see the map on page xviii).

[22]Light, barge-like rowboats used chiefly on rivers.

[23]Boat carried or towed by a ship; ship's boat.

weather, in the open air, in the burning sun, and upon the hard boards, and to dress our meat, and to carry all manner of furniture in them. Wherewith they were so pestered[24] and unsavoury, that what with victuals being most fish, with the wet clothes of so many men thrust together, and the heat of the sun, I will undertake there was never any prison in *England* that could be found more unsavoury and loathsome, especially to myself, who had for many years before been dieted and cared for in a sort far differing.

If Captain *Preston* had not been persuaded that he should have come too late to *Trinidad* to have found us there (for the month was expired which I promised to tarry for him there ere he could recover the coast of *Spain*) but that it had pleased God he might have joined with us, and that we had entered the country but some ten days sooner ere the rivers were overflown, we had adventured either to have gone to the great city of *Manoa*, or at least taken so many of the other cities and towns nearer at hand, as would have made a royal return. But it pleased not God so much to favour me at this time. If it shall be my lot to prosecute the same, I shall willingly spend my life therein. And if any else shall be enabled thereunto, and conquer the same, I assure him thus much: He shall perform more than ever was done in *Mexico* by *Cortez*, or in *Peru* by *Pizarro*, whereof the one conquered the empire of *Mutezuma*, the other of *Guascar* and *Atabalipa*.[25] And whatsoever prince shall possess it, that prince shall be lord of more gold, and of a more beautiful empire, and of more cities and people, than either the king of *Spain* or the great *Turk*.[26]

But because there may arise many doubts, and how this empire of *Guiana* is become so populous, and adorned with so many great cities, towns, temples, and treasures, I thought good to make it known that the emperor now reigning is descended from those magnificent princes of *Peru* of whose large territories, of whose policies, conquests, edifices, and riches, *Pedro de Cieza*, *Francisco Lopez*, and others have written large discourses.[27] For when *Francisco Pizarro*, *Diego Almagro* and others conquered the said empire of *Peru*, and had put to

[24]Crowded or overloaded.

[25]The references are to Hernán Cortés, the conqueror of the Aztec Empire of Montezuma II, and Francisco Pizarro, the conqueror of the Inca Empire of Huáscar and Atahualpa.

[26]The Ottoman emperor, who in 1596 was Murad III.

[27]Ralegh refers to the well-known accounts of Pedro de Cieza de Léon, *Chronica del Peru* (1553), and Francisco López de Gómara, *Istoria de las Indias* (1552) and *Crónica de la conquista de Nueva España* (1552).

death *Atabalipa*, son to *Guaynacapa*, which *Atabalipa* had formerly caused his eldest brother *Guascar* to be slain, one of the younger sons of *Guaynacapa* fled out of *Peru*, and took with him many thousands of those soldiers of the empire called *Orejones*,[28] and with those and many others which followed him, he vanquished all that tract and valley of *America* which is situate between the great river of *Amazones* and *Baraquan*, otherwise called *Orenoque* and *Marañon*.

The empire of *Guiana* is directly east from *Peru* towards the sea, and lieth under the equinoctial line;[29] and it hath more abundance of gold than any part of *Peru*, and as many or more great cities than ever *Peru* had when it flourished most. It is governed by the same laws, and the emperor and people observe the same religion, and the same form and policies in government as were used in *Peru*, not differing in any part. And as I have been assured by such of the Spaniards as have seen *Manoa*, the imperial city of *Guiana*, which the Spaniards call *el Dorado*, that for the greatness, for the riches, and for the excellent seat, it far exceedeth any of the world, at least of so much of the world as is known to the Spanish nation. It is founded upon a lake of salt water of 200 leagues long, like unto *Mare Caspium*.[30] And if we compare it to that of *Peru*, and but read the report of *Francisco Lopez* and others, it will seem more than credible; and because we may judge of the one by the other, I thought good to insert part of the 120 chapter of *Lopez* in his general history of the *Indies*, wherein he describeth the court and magnificence of *Guaynacapa*, ancestor to the emperor of *Guiana*, whose very words are these:

"Todo el servicio de su casa, mesa, y cocina era de oro y de plata, y cuando menos de plata y cobre, por mas recio. Tenia en su recamara estatuas huecas de oro, que parescian gigantes, y las figuras al propio y tamaño de cuantos animales, aves, arboles, y yerbas produce la tierra, y de cuantos peces cria la mar y agua de sus reynos. Tenia asimesmo sogas, costales, cestas, y troxes de oro y plata; rimeros de palos de oro, que pareciesen leña rajada para quemar. En fin no habia cosa en su tierra, que no la tuviese de oro contrahecha; y aun dizen, que tenian los Incas un verjel en una isla cerca de la Puna, donde se

---

[28]"Having large ears," a name that recognized the sizable ear ornaments worn by Inca warriors, which marked their elite status.

[29]Equator.

[30]The Caspian Sea, which, at 143,000 square miles, is the world's largest inland body of water. The belief that a sizable lake occupied the interior of Guiana persisted into the nineteenth century, suggested perhaps by the annual flooding of the savannas.

iban a holgar, cuando querian mar, que tenia la hortaliza, las flores, y arboles de oro y plata; invencion y grandeza hasta entonces nunca vista. Allende de todo esto, tenia infinitisima cantidad de plata y oro por labrar en el Cuzco, que se perdio por la muerte de Guascar; ca los Indios lo escondieron, viendo que los Españoles se lo tomaban, y enviaban a España." That is, "All the vessels of his house, table, and kitchen were of gold and silver, and the meanest of silver and copper for strength and hardness of metal. He had in his wardrobe hollow statues of gold which seemed giants, and the figures in proportion and bigness of all the beasts, birds, trees, and herbs that the earth bringeth forth; and of all the fishes that the sea or waters of his kingdom breedeth. He had also ropes, budgets, chests, and troughs of gold and silver, heaps of billets of gold, that seemed wood, marked out to burn. Finally, there was nothing in his country whereof he had not the counterfeit in gold. Yea, and they say, the *Incas* had a garden of pleasure in an island near *Puna*, where they went to recreate themselves, when they would take the air of the sea, which had all kinds of garden herbs, flowers, and trees of gold and silver, an invention and magnificence till then never seen. Besides all this, he had an infinite quantity of silver and gold unwrought in *Cuzco*, which was lost by the death of *Guascar*, for the Indians hid it, seeing that the Spaniards took it, and sent it into *Spain*."

And in the 117 chapter, *Francisco Pizarro* caused the gold and silver of *Atabalipa* to be weighed after he had taken it, which *Lopez* setteth down in these words following: "Hallaron cincuenta y dos mil marcos de buena plata, y un millon y trecientos y veinte y seis mil y quinientos pesos de oro." Which is, "They found 52,000 marks of good silver, and 1,326,500 *pesos* of gold." Now, although these reports may seem strange, yet if we consider the many millions which are daily brought out of *Peru* into *Spain*, we may easily believe the same. For we find that by the abundant treasure of that country the Spanish king vexes all the princes of *Europe*, and is become, in a few years, from a poor king of *Castile*, the greatest monarch of this part of the world, and likely every day to increase if other princes forslow[31] the good occasions offered, and suffer him to add this empire to the rest, which by far exceedeth all the rest. If his gold now endanger us, he will then be unresistible. Such of the Spaniards as afterward endeavoured the conquest thereof (whereof there have been many, as shall be declared hereafter) thought that this *Inca*, of whom this emperor now living is

[31] Neglect or put off.

descended, took his way by the river of *Amazones*, by that branch which is called *Papamene*. For by that way followed Oreliano (by the commandment of the Marqués *Pizarro*) in the year 1542, whose name the river also beareth this day, which is also by others called *Marañon*, although *Andrew Thevet* doth affirm that between *Marañon* and *Amazones* there are 120 leagues; but sure it is that those rivers have one head and beginning, and the *Marañon*, which *Thevet* describeth, is but a branch of *Amazones* or *Oreliano*, of which I will speak more in another place.[32] It was also attempted by *Diego Ordace* but whether before *Oreliano* or after I know not; but it is now little less than 70 years since that *Ordace*, a knight of the Order of *Santiago*, attempted the same; and it was in the year 1542 that *Oreliano* discovered the river of *Amazones*; but the first that ever saw *Manoa* was *Juan Martinez*,[33] master of the munition to *Ordace*. At a port called *Morequito* in *Guiana*, there lieth at this day a great anchor of *Ordace*'s ship. And this port is some 300 miles within the land, upon the great river of Orenoque. I rested at this port four days, twenty days after I left the ships at *Curiapan*.

The relation of this *Martinez* (who was the first that discovered *Manoa*), his success, and end, is to be seen in the Chancery of *St. Juan de Puerto Rico*, whereof *Berreo* had a copy, which appeared to be the greatest encouragement as well to *Berreo* as to others that formerly attempted the discovery and conquest. *Oreliano*, after he failed of the discovery of *Guiana* by the said river of *Amazones*, passed into *Spain*, and there obtained a patent of the king for the invasion and conquest, but died by sea about the Islands; and his fleet being severed by tempest, the action for that time proceeded not. *Diego Ordace* followed the enterprise, and departed *Spain* with 600 soldiers and thirty horse. Who, arriving on the coast of *Guiana*, was slain in a mutiny, with the most part of such as favoured him, as also of the rebellious part, insomuch as his ships perished and few or none returned; neither was it certainly known what became of the said *Ordace* until *Berreo* found the anchor of his ship in the river of *Orenoque*; but

---

[32]Ralegh's brisk recitation of the journeys of Gonzalo Pizarro and his lieutenant, Francisco de Orellana ("Oreliano"), along with the summary that follows of attempts by Diego de Ordás ("Ordace"), Pedro de Ursúa ("Osua," mentioned later), and others to navigate the Orinoco and other rivers of the region, contain numerous inaccuracies (geographical and historical). This is a reflection of both the uneven flow of information pertaining to Spanish exploration (intentionally kept out of enemy hands) and Ralegh's rapid method of composition (sometimes from memory and with minimal revision). Note that the thousand-mile-long Marañón flows through Peru before turning into the Amazon, in which form it crosses Brazil and empties into the Atlantic.

[33]Juan Martínez (or Martin) de Albujar.

it was supposed, and so it is written by *Lopez*, that he perished on the seas, and of other writers diversely conceived and reported. And hereof it came that *Martinez* entered so far within the land and arrived at that city of *Inca* the emperor; for it chanced that while *Ordace* with his army rested at the port of *Morequito* (who was either the first or second that attempted *Guiana*), by some negligence the whole store of powder provided for the service was set on fire, and *Martinez*, having the chief charge, was condemned by the general *Ordace* to be executed forthwith. *Martinez*, being much favoured by the soldiers, had all the means possible procured for his life; but it could not be obtained in other sort than this: that he should be set into a *canoa* alone, without any victual, only with his arms, and so turned loose into the great river. But it pleased God that the *canoa* was carried down the stream, and that certain of the *Guianians* met it the same evening; and, having not at any time seen any Christian nor any man of that colour, they carried *Martinez* into the land to be wondered at, and so from town to town, until he came to the great city of *Manoa*, the seat and residence of *Inca* the emperor. The emperor, after he had beheld him, knew him to be a Christian (for it was not long before that his brethren *Guascar* and *Atabalipa* were vanquished by the Spaniards in *Peru*) and caused him to be lodged in his palace and well entertained. He lived seven months in *Manoa*, but [was] not suffered to wander into the country anywhere. He was also brought thither all the way blindfolded, led by the Indians, until he came to the entrance of *Manoa* itself, and was fourteen or fifteen days in the passage. He avowed at his death that he entered the city at noon, and then they uncovered his face; and that he travelled all that day till night through the city, and the next day from sun rising to sun setting, ere he came to the palace of *Inca*. After that *Martinez* had lived seven months in *Manoa*, and began to understand the language of the country, *Inca* asked him whether he desired to return into his own country, or would willingly abide with him. But *Martinez*, not desirous to stay, obtained the favour of *Inca* to depart; with whom he sent divers *Guianians* to conduct him to the river of *Orenoque*, all loaden with as much gold as they could carry, which he gave to *Martinez* at his departure. But when he was arrived near the river's side, the borderers[34] which are called *Orenoqueponi*[35] robbed him and his *Guianians* of all the treasure (the borderers being at that time at wars with *Inca* and not conquered) save only of two great bottles of gourds, which were filled

---

[34]Those living outside Guiana in adjoining territory.
[35]"Those living on the Orinoco."

with beads of gold curiously wrought, which those *Orenoqueponi* thought had been no other thing than his drink or meat or grain for food, with which *Martinez* had liberty to pass. And so in *canoas* he fell down from the river of *Orenoque* to *Trinidad*, and from thence to *Margarita*, and so to *St. Juan de Puerto Rico*, where, remaining a long time for passage into *Spain*, he died. In the time of his extreme sickness, and when he was without hope of life, receiving the *Sacrament* at the hands of his confessor, he delivered these things, with the relation of his travels, and also called for his *calabazas* or gourds of the gold beads, which he gave to the church and friars, to be prayed for.

This *Martinez* was he that christened the city of *Manoa* by the name of *El Dorado*, as *Berreo* informed me upon this occasion.[36] Those *Guianians*, and also the borderers, and all other in that tract which I have seen, are marvellous great drunkards, in which vice I think no nation can compare with them; and at the times of their solemn feasts, when the emperor carouseth with his captains, tributaries, and governors, the manner is thus. All those that pledge him are first stripped naked and their bodies anointed all over with a kind of white *balsam* (by them called *curcai*),[37] of which there is great plenty, and yet very dear amongst them, and it is of all other the most precious, whereof we have had good experience. When they are anointed all over, certain servants of the emperor, having prepared gold made into fine powder, blow it through hollow canes upon their naked bodies, until they be all shining from the foot to the head;[38] and in this sort they sit drinking by twenties and hundreds, and continue in drunkenness sometimes six or seven days together. The same is also confirmed by a letter written into *Spain* which was intercepted, which Master *Robert Dudley* told me he had seen.[39] Upon this sight, and for the abundance of gold which he saw in the city, the images of gold in their temples, the plates, armours, and shields of gold which they use in the wars, he called it *El Dorado*.

[36]This is a critical moment in the El Dorado legend: the identification by Ralegh (via Berreo, who reported the adventures of Martínez) of a golden king (*el dorado*) with the city of Manoa in Guiana, which will come to be called El Dorado.

[37]This is *Copaifera officinalis*, or *curucai*, whose oil (or *balsam*, as Ralegh calls it) is mixed with annatto to produce a body paint that also had medicinal uses and would later become a trade commodity.

[38]See Document 3, Figure 8.

[39]Dudley, the illegitimate son of Robert Dudley, first earl of Leicester (and a rival of Ralegh), voyaged to the region just before Ralegh, arriving in Trinidad on February 1, 1595. He stayed for nearly six weeks before returning to England with stories (yet no evidence) of abundant gold. Ralegh arrived in Trinidad a mere ten days after Dudley's departure on March 10, 1595.

After *Oreliano*, who was employed by *Pizarro* (afterwards Marqués *Pizarro*, conqueror and governor of Peru), and the death of *Ordace* and *Martinez*, one *Pedro de Osua*, a knight of *Navarre*, attempted *Guiana*, taking his way from *Peru*, and built his brigantines upon a river called *Oia*, which riseth to the southward of *Quito*, and is very great.[40] This river falleth into *Amazones*, by which *Osua* with his companies descended and came out of that province which is called *Mutylones*,[41] and it seemeth to me that this empire is reserved for her Majesty and the English nation, by reason of the hard success which all these and other Spaniards found in attempting the same, whereof I will speak briefly, though impertinent in some sort to my purpose. This *Pedro de Osua* had among his troops a Biscayan called *Agiri*, a man meanly born, [who] bore no other office than a sergeant or *alferez*: but after certain months, when the soldiers were grieved with travels and consumed with famine, and that no entrance could be found by the branches or body of *Amazones*, this *Agiri* raised a mutiny, of which he made himself the head, and so prevailed as he put *Osua* to the sword and all his followers, taking on him the whole charge and commandment, with a purpose not only to make himself emperor of *Guiana*, but also of *Peru* and of all that side of the *West Indies*. He had of his party 700 soldiers, and of those many promised to draw in other captains and companies, to deliver up towns and forts in *Peru*; but neither finding by the said river any passage into *Guiana*, nor any possibility to return towards *Peru* by the same *Amazones*, by reason that the descent of the river made so great a current, he was enforced to disemboque[42] at the mouth of the said *Amazones*, which cannot be less than 1,000 leagues from the place where they embarked. From thence he coasted the land till he arrived at *Margarita* to the north of *Mompatar*, which is at this day called *Puerto de Tyranno*, for that he there slew *Don Juan de Villa Andreda*, Governor of *Margarita*, who was father to *Don Juan Sarmiento*, Governor of *Margarita* when Sir *John Burgh* landed there and attempted the island. *Agiri* put to the sword all others in the island that refused to be of his party, and took with him certain *cemerones*[43] and other desperate companions. From thence he went to *Cumana* and there slew the governor, and dealt in all as at

---

[40]The story of Pedro de Ursúa ("Osua"), who undertook his failed journey in 1560–1561 with the volatile Lope de Aguirre ("Agiri"), has been fictionalized in the film *Aguirre, der Zorn Gottes* (1972), made by the great German director Werner Herzog.

[41]*Motilones*, or hairless, so named for the inhabitants' cropped or shaved heads.

[42]Disembark.

[43]*Cimarrones*: runaway slaves.

Margarita. He spoiled all the coast of *Caracas* and the province of *Venezuela* and of *Rio de la Hacha*; and, as I remember, it was the same year that Sir *John Hawkins* sailed to *St. Juan de Ullua* in the *Jesus* of *Lubeck*,[44] for himself told me that he met with such a one upon the coast that rebelled, and had sailed down all the river of *Amazones*. *Agiri* from thence landed about *Santa Marta* and sacked it also, putting to death so many as refused to be his followers, purposing to invade *Nuevo Reyno de Granada* and to sack *Pamplona, Merida, Lagrita, Tunja*, and the rest of the cities of *Nuevo Reyno*, and from thence again to enter *Peru*; but in a fight in the said *Nuevo Reyno* he was overthrown, and, finding no way to escape, he first put to the sword his own children, foretelling them that they should not live to be defamed or upbraided by the *Spaniards* after his death, who would have termed them the children of a traitor or tyrant; and that, sithence[45] he could not make them princes, he would yet deliver them from shame and reproach. These were the ends and tragedies of *Oreliano, Ordace, Osua, Martinez*, and *Agiri*. After these followed *Jeronimo Ortal de Saragosa*, with 130 soldiers, who, failing his entrance by sea, was cast with the current on the coast of *Paria*, and peopled about *S. Miguel de Neveri*. It was then attempted by *Don Pedro de Silva*, a Portuguese of the family of *Ruy Gomez de Silva*, and by the favour which *Ruy Gomes* had with the king, he was set out. But he also shot wide of the mark; for being departed from *Spain* with his fleet, he entered by *Marañon* or *Amazones*, where by the nations of the river and by the *Amazones*, he was utterly overthrown, and himself and all his army defeated; only seven escaped, and of those but two returned.

After him came *Pedro Hernandez de Serpa*, and landed at *Cumana* in the *West Indies*, taking his journey by land towards *Orenoque*, which may be some 120 leagues; but ere he came to the borders of the said river, he was set upon by a nation of Indians called *Wikiri*,[46] and overthrown in sort, that of 300 soldiers, horsemen, many Indians, and *Negroes*, there returned but eighteen. Others affirm that he was defeated in the very entrance of *Guiana*, at the first civil town of the empire called *Macureguarai*. Captain *Preston*, in taking *Santiago de Leon* (which was by him and his companies very resolutely performed, being a great town, and far within the land), held a gentleman prisoner, who died in his ship, that was one of the company of *Her-*

---

[44] Hawkins was in the region in 1567–1568.
[45] Since.
[46] Guayqueries.

nandez de Serpa, and saved among those that escaped; who witnessed what opinion is held among the Spaniards thereabouts of the great riches of *Guiana*, and *El Dorado*, the city of *Inca*. Another Spaniard was brought aboard me by Captain *Preston*, who told me in the hearing of himself and divers other gentlemen, that he met with *Berreo's* campmaster at *Caracas*, when he came from the borders of *Guiana*, and that he saw with him forty of most pure plates of gold, curiously wrought, and swords of *Guiana* decked and inlaid with gold, feathers garnished with gold, and divers rarities, which he carried to the Spanish king.[47]

After *Hernandez de Serpa*, it was undertaken by the *Adelantado, Don Gonzalez Ximenes de Quesada*, who was one of the chiefest in the conquest of *Nuevo Reyno*, whose daughter and heir *Don Antonio de Berreo* married. *Gonzales* sought the passage also by the river called *Papamene*, which riseth by *Quito*, in *Peru*, and runneth southeast 100 leagues, and then falleth into *Amazones*. But he also, failing the entrance, returned with the loss of much labour and cost. I took one Captain *George*, a Spaniard, that followed *Gonzalez* in this enterprise. *Gonzalez* gave his daughter to *Berreo*, taking his oath and honour to follow the enterprise to the last of his substance and life; who since, as he hath sworn to me, hath spent 300,000 ducats in the same, and yet never could enter so far into the land as myself with that poor troop, or rather a handful of men, being in all about 100 gentlemen, soldiers, rowers, boat-keepers, boys, and of all sorts; neither could any of the forepassed undertakers, nor *Berreo* himself, discover the country, till now lately by conference with an ancient king called *Carapana*[48] he got the true light thereof. For *Berreo* came about 1,500 miles ere he understood aught, or could find any passage or entrance into any part thereof; yet he had experience of all these fore-named, and divers others, and was persuaded of their errors and mistakings. *Berreo* sought it by the river *Cassanar*, which falleth into a great river called *Pato*; *Pato* falleth into *Meta*, and *Meta* into *Baraquan*, which is also called *Orenoque*.

He took his journey from *Nuevo Reyno de Granada*, where he dwelt, having the inheritance of *Gonzalez Ximenes* in those parts; he was

---

[47]This would have been Domingo de Vera, who took formal possession of Guiana on Berrio's behalf. His report to the Spanish court impressed the crown—as did the precious metals and "divers rarities"—and convinced the court to support a subsequent colonizing expedition, which arrived after Ralegh's visit.

[48]The name means "the Mosquito."

followed with 700 horses, he drove with him 1,000 head of cattle, he had also many women, Indians, and slaves. How all these rivers cross and encounter, how the country lieth and is bordered, the passage of *Ximenes* and of *Berreo*, mine own discovery, and the way that I entered, with all the rest of the nations and rivers, your lordship shall receive in a large chart or map, which I have not yet finished, and which I shall most humbly pray your lordship to secrete, and not to suffer it to pass your own hands;[49] for by a draught thereof all may be prevented by other nations. For I know it is this very year sought by the French, although by the way that they now take, I fear it not much. It was also told me ere I departed *England*, that *Villiers*, the Admiral, was in preparation for the planting of *Amazones*, to which river the French have made divers voyages, and returned much gold and other rarities. I spake with a captain of a French ship that came from thence, his ship riding in *Falmouth* the same year that my ships came first from Virginia. There was another this year in *Helford*, that also came from thence, and had been fourteen months at an anchor in *Amazones*, which were both very rich.

Although, as I am persuaded, *Guiana* cannot be entered that way, yet no doubt the trade of gold from thence passeth by branches of rivers into the river of *Amazones*, and so it doth on every hand far from the country itself; for those Indians of *Trinidad* have plates of gold from *Guiana*, and those cannibals of *Dominica* which dwell in the islands by which our ships pass yearly to the *West Indies*, also the Indians of *Paria*, those Indians called *Tucaris, Chochi, Apotomios, Cumanagotos*, and all those other nations inhabiting near about the mountains that run from *Paria* through the province of *Venezuela*, and in *Maracapana*, and the cannibals of *Guanipa*, the Indians called *Assawai, Coaca, Ajai*, and the rest (all which shall be described in my description as they are situate) have plates of gold of *Guiana*. And upon the river of *Amazones*, *Thevet* writeth that the people wear *croissants*[50] of gold, for of that form the *Guianians* most commonly make them; so as from *Dominica* to *Amazones*, which is above 250 leagues, all the chief Indians in all parts wear of those plates of *Guiana*. Undoubtedly those that trade [with the] *Amazones* return much gold, which (as is aforesaid) cometh by trade from *Guiana*, by some branch

---

[49] A manuscript map housed in the British Library is attributed to Ralegh, although it might also derive from a copy of an original, with additions from Lawrence Keymis's journey of 1596.

[50] Crescents: the shape of the waxing or waning moon.

of a river that falleth from the country into *Amazones*, and either it is by the river which passeth by the nations called *Tisnados*, or by *Caripuna*.

I made enquiry amongst the most ancient and best travelled of the *Orenoqueponi*, and I had knowledge of all the rivers between *Orenoque* and *Amazones*, and was very desirous to understand the truth of those warlike women, because of some it is believed, of others not. And though I digress from my purpose, yet I will set down what hath been delivered me for truth of those women, and I spake with a *cacique*, or lord of people, that told me he had been in the river, and beyond it also. The nations of these women are on the south side of the river in the provinces of *Topago*,[51] and their chiefest strengths and retracts[52] are in the islands situate on the south side of the entrance, some 60 leagues within the mouth of the said river. The memories of the like women are very ancient as well in *Africa* as in *Asia*. In *Africa* those that had *Medusa* for queen; others in *Scythia*, near the rivers of *Tanais* and *Thermodon*. We find also that *Lampedo* and *Marthesia* were queens of the *Amazones*. In many histories they are verified to have been, and in divers ages and provinces. But they which are not far from *Guiana* do accompany[53] with men but once in a year, and for the time of one month, which I gather by their relation to be in April. At that time all the kings of the borders assemble, and the queens of the *Amazones*; and after the queens have chosen, the rest cast lots for their valentines. This one month they feast, dance, and drink of their wines in abundance; and the moon being done, they all depart to their own provinces. If they conceive and be delivered of a son, they return him to the father; if of a daughter, they nourish it and retain it. And as many as have daughters send unto the begetters a present, all being desirous to increase their own sex and kind. But that they cut of the right dug[54] of the breast I do not find to be true. It was further told me that if in the wars they took any prisoners that they used to accompany with those also at what time soever; but in the end for certain they put them to death. For they are said to be very cruel and bloodthirsty, especially to such as offer to invade their territories. These *Amazones* have likewise great store of these plates of gold, which they recover by exchange chiefly for a kind of green stones, which the

[51]The Tapajós River, a tributary of the Amazon.
[52]Places of retreat or refuge.
[53]Keep company or cohabit.
[54]Nipple.

Spaniards call *piedras hijadas*, and we use for spleen-stones;[55] and for the disease of the stone[56] we also esteem them. Of these I saw divers in *Guiana*; and commonly every king or *cacique* hath one, which their wives for the most part wear, and they esteem them as great jewels.

But to return to the enterprise of *Berreo*, who (as I have said) departed from *Nuevo Reyno* with 700 horses, besides the provisions above rehearsed. He descended by the river called *Cassanar*, which riseth in *Nuevo Reyno* out of the mountains by the city of *Tunja*, from which mountain also springeth *Pato*; both which fall into the great river of *Meta*, and *Meta* riseth from a mountain joining to *Pamplona*, in the same *Nuevo Reyno de Granada*. These, as also *Guaiare*, which issueth out of the mountains by *Timana*, fall all into *Baraquan*, and are but of his heads; for at their coming together they lose their names, and *Baraquan* farther down is also rebaptized by the name of *Orenoque*. On the other side of the city and hills of *Timana* riseth *Rio Grande*, which falleth into the sea by *Santa Marta*. By *Cassanar* first, and so into *Meta*, *Berreo* passed, keeping his horsemen on the banks, where the country served them for to march; and where otherwise, he was driven to embark them in boats which he builded for the purpose, and so came with the current down the river of *Meta*, and so into *Baraquan*. After he entered that great and mighty river, he began daily to lose of his companies both men and horses; for it is in many places violently swift, and hath forcible eddies, many sands, and divers islands sharp pointed with rocks. But after one whole year, journeying for the most part by river, and the rest by land, he grew daily to fewer numbers; for both by sickness and by encountering with the people of those regions through which he travelled, his companies were much wasted, especially by divers encounters with the *Amapaians*. And in all this time he never could learn of any passage into *Guiana*, nor any news or fame thereof, until he came to a further border of the said *Amapaia*, eight days' journey from the river *Caroli*, which was the furthest river that we entered. Among those of *Amapaia*, *Guiana* was famous; but few of these people accosted *Berreo*, or would trade with him the first three months of the six which he sojourned there. This *Amapaia* is also marvellous rich in gold (as both *Berreo* confessed, and those of *Guiana* with whom I had most conference) and is situate upon *Orenoque* also. In this country *Berreo* lost sixty of his best soldiers, and most of all his horses that remained of his former year's

---

[55]Stones thought to cure disorders of the spleen.
[56]Gallstones.

travel. But in the end, after divers encounters with those nations, they grew to peace, and they presented *Berreo* with ten images of fine gold among divers other plates and *croissants*, which, as he swore to me and divers other gentlemen, were so curiously wrought, as he had not seen the like either in *Italy*, *Spain*, or the *Low Countries*; and he was resolved that when they came to the hands of the Spanish king, to whom he had sent them by his campmaster, they would appear very admirable, especially being wrought by such a nation as had no iron instruments at all, nor any of those helps which our goldsmiths have to work withal. The particular name of the people in *Amapaia* which gave him these pieces are called *Anebas*, and the river of *Orenoque* at that place is above twelve English miles broad,[57] which may be from his outfall into the sea 700 or 800 miles.

This province of *Amapaia* is a very low and a marish[58] ground near the river; and by reason of the red water which issueth out in small branches through the fenny and boggy ground, there breed divers poisonful worms and serpents. And the Spaniards not suspecting, nor in any sort foreknowing the danger, were infected with a grievous kind of flux[59] by drinking thereof, and even the very horses poisoned therewith; insomuch as at the end of the six months that they abode there, of all their troops there were not left above 120 soldiers, and neither horse nor cattle. For *Berreo* hoped to have found *Guiana* by 1,000 miles nearer than it fell out to be in the end; by means whereof they sustained much want and much hunger, oppressed with grievous diseases, and all the miseries that could be imagined. I demanded of those in *Guiana* that had travelled *Amapaia* how they lived with that tawny or red water when they travelled thither; and they told me that after the sun was near the middle of the sky, they used to fill their pots and pitchers with that water, but either before that time or towards the setting of the sun it was dangerous to drink of, and in the night strong poison. I learned also of divers other rivers of that nature among them, which were also (while the sun was in the meridian) very safe to drink, and in the morning, evening, and night, wonderful dangerous and infective. From this province *Berreo* hastened away as soon as the spring and beginning of summer appeared, and sought his entrance

---

[57]This is inaccurate—the river may be two to three miles wide at this point—and perhaps a misprint ("12" in the original instead of "2").

[58]Marshy.

[59]Flowing, or flow, which Ralegh uses in a medical sense: an abnormal flow of blood or excrement from the bowels (as with dysentery) or other organs; a discharge of fluids, otherwise, from the eyes, mouth, and so on.

on the borders of *Orenoque* on the south side; but there ran a ledge of so high and impassable mountains, as he was not able by any means to march over them, continuing from the east sea into which *Orenoque* falleth, even to *Quito* in *Peru*. Neither had he means to carry victual or munition over those craggy, high, and fast hills, being all woody, and those so thick and spiny, and so full of prickles, thorns, and briars, as it is impossible to creep thorough them. He had also neither friendship among the people, nor any interpreter to persuade or treat with them; and more to his disadvantage, the *caciques* and kings of *Amapaia* had given knowledge of his purpose to the *Guianians*, and that he sought to sack and conquer the empire, for the hope of their so great abundance and quantities of gold. He passed by the mouths of many great rivers, which fell into *Orenoque* both from the north and south, which I forbear to name for tediousness, and because they are more pleasing in describing than reading.

Berreo affirmed that there fell a hundred rivers into *Orenoque* from the north and south, whereof the least was as big as *Rio Grande*, that passed between *Popayan* and *Nuevo Reyno de Granada* (*Rio Grande* being esteemed one of the renowned rivers in all the *West Indies*, and numbered among the great rivers of the world). But he knew not the names of any of these, but *Caroli* only, neither from what nations they descended, neither to what provinces they led; for he had no means to discourse with the inhabitants at any time. Neither was he curious in these things, being utterly unlearned, and not knowing the east from the west. But of all these I got some knowledge, and of many more, partly by mine own travel, and the rest by conference; of someone I learned one, of others the rest, having with me an Indian that spake many languages, and that of *Guiana* naturally.[60] I sought out all the aged men, and such as were greatest travellers. And by the one and the other I came to understand the situations, the rivers, the kingdoms from the east sea to the borders of *Peru*, and from *Orenoque* southward as far as *Amazones* or *Marañon*, and the regions of *Maria Tamball*, and of all the kings of provinces, and captains of towns and villages, how they stood in terms of peace or war, and which were friends or enemies the one with the other; without which there can be neither entrance nor conquest in those parts, nor elsewhere. For by

---

[60] Ralegh's references to native informants, and speakers of Carib languages in particular, provide the best evidence of his reliance on indigenous knowledge, without which he probably could not have accomplished all that he did. "Martin the Arwacan," an Indian pilot, is singled out for recognition later in the narrative (page 81).

the dissension between *Guascar* and *Atabalipa*, *Pizarro* conquered *Peru*, and by the hatred that the *Tlaxcalans* bore to *Mutezuma*, *Cortez* was victorious over *Mexico*; without which both the one and the other had failed of their enterprise, and of the great honour and riches, which they attained unto.

Now *Berreo* began to grow into despair, and looked for no other success than his predecessor in this enterprise; until such time as he arrived at the province of *Emeria* towards the east sea and mouth of the river, where he found a nation of people very favourable, and the country full of all manner of victual. The king of this land is called *Carapana*, a man very wise, subtle, and of great experience, being little less than one hundred years old. In his youth he was sent by his father into the island of *Trinidad*, by reason of civil war among themselves, and was bred at a village in that island, called *Parico*. At that place in his youth he had seen many Christians, both French and Spanish, and went divers times with the Indians of *Trinidad* to *Margarita* and *Cumaná*, in the *West Indies* (for both those places have ever been relieved with victual from *Trinidad*), by reason whereof he grew of more understanding, and noted the difference of the nations, comparing the strength and arms of his country with those of the Christians, and ever after temporized[61] so as whosoever else did amiss, or was wasted by contention, *Carapana* kept himself and his country in quiet and plenty. He also held peace with the *Caribs* or cannibals, his neighbours, and had free trade with all nations, whosoever else had war.

Berreo sojourned and rested his weak troop in the town of *Carapana* six weeks, and from him learned the way and passage to *Guiana*, and the riches and magnificence thereof. But being then utterly disable to proceed, he determined to try his fortune another year, when he had renewed his provisions, and regathered more force, which he hoped for as well out of *Spain* as from *Nuevo Reyno*, where he had left his son *Don Antonio Ximenes* to second him upon the first notice given of his entrance; and so for the present embarked himself in *canoas*, and by the branches of *Orenoque* arrived at *Trinidad*, having from *Carapana* sufficient pilots to conduct him. From *Trinidad* he coasted *Paria*, and so recovered *Margarita*; and having made relation to *Don Juan Sarmiento*, the Governor, of his proceeding, and persuaded him of the riches of *Guiana*, he obtained from thence fifty soldiers, promising presently to return to *Carapana*, and

---

[61] Negotiated, arranged, or came to terms with.

so into *Guiana*. But *Berreo* meant nothing less at that time; for he wanted many provisions necessary for such an enterprise, and therefore, departing from *Margarita*, seated himself in *Trinidad*, and from thence sent his campmaster and his sergeant-major back to the borders to discover the nearest passage into the empire, as also to treat with the borderers, and to draw them to his party and love; without which, he knew he could neither pass safely, nor in any sort be relieved with victual or aught else. *Carapana* directed his company to a king called *Morequito*, assuring them that no man could deliver so much of *Guiana* as *Morequito* could, and that his dwelling was but five days' journey from *Macureguarai*, the first civil town of *Guiana*.

Now your lordship shall understand that this *Morequito*, one of the greatest lords or kings of the borders of *Guiana*, had two or three years before been at *Cumaná* and at *Margarita*, in the *West Indies*, with great store of plates of gold, which he carried to exchange for such other things as he wanted in his own country, and was daily feasted, and presented by the governors of those places, and held amongst them some two months. In which time one *Vides*, Governor of *Cumaná*, won him to be his conductor into *Guiana*, being allured by those *croissants* and images of gold which he brought with him to trade, as also by the ancient fame and magnificence of *El Dorado*; whereupon *Vides* sent into *Spain* for a patent to discover and conquer *Guiana*, not knowing of the precedence of *Berreo's* patent; which, as *Berreo* affirmeth, was signed before that of *Vides*. So as when *Vides* understood of *Berreo*, and that he had made entrance into that territory, and foregone his desire and hope, it was verily thought that *Vides* practiced with *Morequito* to hinder and disturb *Berreo* in all he could, and not to suffer him to enter through his seignory, nor any of his companies, neither to victual, nor guide them in any sort. For *Vides*, Governor of *Cumaná*, and *Berreo* were become mortal enemies, as well for that *Berreo*, and had gotten *Trinidad* into his patent with *Guiana*, as also in that he was by *Berreo* prevented in the journey of *Guiana* itself. Howsoever it was, I know not, but *Morequito* for a time dissembled his disposition, suffered [ten] Spaniards and a friar (which *Berreo* had sent to discover *Manoa*) to travel through his country, gave them a guide for *Macureguarai*, the first town of civil and apparelled people, from whence they had other guides to bring them to *Manoa*, the great city of *Inca*; and being furnished with those things, which they had learned of *Carapana* were of most price in *Guiana*, went onward, and in eleven days arrived at *Manoa*, as *Berreo* affirmeth for certain; although I could not be assured thereof by the lord which now governeth the province of *Morequito*, for he told me that they got all the gold they had in other towns on this side [of] *Manoa*, there being many very great and rich, and (as he said) built like the towns of Christians, with many rooms.

When these ten Spaniards were returned, and ready to put out of the border of *Aromaia*, the people of *Morequito* set upon them, and slew them all but one that swam the river, and took from them to the value of 40,000 *pesos* of gold; and, as it is written in the story of Job, one only lived to bring the news to *Berreo*, that both his nine soldiers and holy father were benighted[62] in the said province. I myself spake with the captains of *Morequito* that slew them, and was at the place where it was executed. *Berreo*, enraged herewithal, sent all the strength he could make into *Aromaia*, to be revenged of him, his people, and country. But *Morequito*, suspecting the same, fled over *Orenoque*, and through the territories of the *Saima* and *Wikiri*, recovered *Cumaná*, where he thought himself very safe with *Vides* the governor. But *Berreo* sending for him in the king's name, and his messengers finding him in the house of one *Fajardo*, on the sudden, ere he was suspected, so as he could not then be conveyed away, *Vides* durst not deny him, as well to avoid the suspicion of the practice, as also for that a holy father was slain by him and his people. *Morequito* offered *Fajardo* the weight of three quintals in gold,[63] to let him escape; but the poor *Guianian*, betrayed on all sides, was delivered to the campmaster of *Berreo*, and was presently executed.

After the death of this *Morequito*, the soldiers of *Berreo* spoiled his territory and took divers prisoners. Among others they took the uncle of *Morequito*, called *Topiawari*, who is now king of *Aromaia* (whose son I brought with me into *England*) and is a man of great understanding and policy; he is above one hundred years old, and yet of a very able body. The Spaniards led him in a chain seventeen days and made him their guide from place to place between his country and *Emeria*, the province of *Carapana* aforesaid, and [he] was at last redeemed for a hundred plates of gold, and divers stones called *piedras hijadas*, or spleen-stones. Now *Berreo*, for executing of *Morequito* and other cruelties, spoils, and slaughters done in *Aromaia*, hath lost the love of the *Orenoqueponi*, and of all the borderers, and dare not send any of his soldiers any further into the land than to *Carapana*, which

---

[62] Killed.

[63] A traditional unit of weight, especially in the Iberian world, equal to a bit more than 100 pounds (thus the offer is in excess of 300 pounds of gold).

he called the port of *Guiana*; but from thence by the help of *Carapana* he had trade further into the country, and always appointed ten Spaniards to reside in *Carapana's* town,[64] by whose favour, and by being conducted by his people, those ten searched the country thereabouts, as well for mines as for other trades and commodities.

They have also gotten a nephew of *Morequito*, whom they have christened and named *Don Juan*, of whom they have great hope, endeavouring by all means to establish him in the said province. Among many other trades, those Spaniards used *canoas* to pass to the rivers of *Barema*, *Pawroma*, and *Dissequebe*, which are on the south side of the mouth of *Orenoque*, and there buy women and children from the *Cannibals*, which are of that barbarous nature, as they will for three or four hatchets sell the sons and daughters of their own brethren and sisters, and for somewhat more even their own daughters. Hereof the Spaniards make great profit; for buying a maid of twelve or thirteen years for three or four hatchets, they sell them again at *Margarita* in the *West Indies* for fifty and a hundred *pesos*, which is so many crowns.[65]

The master of my ship, *John Douglas*, took one of the *canoas* which came laden from thence with people to be sold, and the most of them escaped; yet of those he brought, there was one as well favoured and as well shaped as ever I saw any in *England*; and afterward I saw many of them, which but for their tawny colour may be compared to any in *Europe*. They also trade in those rivers for bread of *cassavi*, of which they buy a hundred pound weight for a knife, and sell it at *Margarita* for ten *pesos*. They also recover great store of cotton, brazil wood, and those beds which they call *hamacas* or brazil beds,[66] wherein in hot countries all the Spaniards use to lie commonly, and in no other, neither did we ourselves while we were there. By means of which trades, for ransom of divers of the *Guianians*, and for exchange of hatchets and knives, *Berreo* recovered some store of gold plates,

[64]This is more than likely the Spanish settlement of Santo Tomé, founded by Berrio a few years earlier.

[65]Whitehead explains that such Carib ("cannibal") slaving had a highly complex native context that was generally lost on the Europeans, the barter of younger members of a community establishing reciprocal obligations with those on the receiving end. See Sir Walter Ralegh, *The Discoverie of the Large, Rich and Bewtiful Empyre of Guiana*, ed. Neil L. Whitehead, American Exploration and Travel Series, vol. 77 (Norman: University of Oklahoma Press, 1997).

[66]Hammocks. Used throughout the Caribbean and in Brazil ("brazil beds"), hammocks were admired by the Europeans, and they provided ready evidence of the excellent crafts (and ingenuity) of the indigenous peoples.

eagles of gold, and images of men and divers birds, and dispatched his campmaster for *Spain* with all that he had gathered, therewith to levy soldiers, and by the show thereof to draw others to the love of the enterprise. And having sent divers images as well of men as beasts, birds, and fishes, so curiously wrought in gold, [he] doubted not but to persuade the king to yield to him some further help, especially for that this land hath never been sacked, the mines never wrought, and in the *Indies* their works were well spent, and the gold drawn out with great labour and charge. He also despatched messengers to his son in *Nuevo Reyno* to levy all the forces he could, and to come down the river *Orenoque* to *Emeria*, the province of *Carapana*, to meet him; he had also sent to *Santiago de Leon* on the coast of the *Caracas*, to buy horses and mules.

After I had thus learned of his proceedings past and purposed, I told him that I had resolved to see *Guiana*, and that it was the end of my journey and the cause of my coming to *Trinidad*, as it was indeed (and for that purpose I sent *Jacob Whiddon* the year before to get intelligence, with whom *Berreo* himself had speech at that time, and remembered how inquisitive *Jacob Whiddon* was of his proceedings, and of the country of *Guiana*). *Berreo* was stricken into a great melancholy and sadness, and used all the arguments he could to dissuade me; and also assured the gentlemen of my company that it would be labour lost, and that they should suffer many miseries if they proceeded. And first he delivered[67] that I could not enter any of the rivers with any bark or pinnace,[68] nor hardly with any ship's boat, it was so low, sandy, and full of flats, and that his companies were daily grounded in their *canoas*, which drew but twelve inches water. He further said that none of the country would come to speak with us, but would all fly; and if we followed them to their dwellings, they would burn their own towns. And besides that, the way was long, the winter at hand, and that the rivers beginning once to swell, it was impossible to stem the current; and that we could not in those small boats by any means carry victuals for half the time, and that (which indeed most discouraged my company) the kings and lords of all the borders of *Guiana* had decreed that none of them should trade with any Christians for gold, because the same would be their own overthrow, and that for the love of gold the Christians meant to conquer and dispossess them of all together.

---

[67] Pronounced or expressed his opinion; discoursed.
[68] Small sailing vessel that would have been too large for the Orinoco delta.

Many and the most of these I found to be true; but yet I, resolving to make trial of whatsoever happened, directed Captain *George Gifford*, my Vice-Admiral, to take the *Lion's Whelp*, and Captain *Caulfield* his bark, to turn to the eastward, against the breeze what they could possible, to recover the mouth of a river called *Capuri*, whose entrance I had before sent Captain *Whiddon* and *John Douglas* the master to discover; who found some nine foot water or better upon the flood, and five at low water; to whom I had given instructions that they should anchor at the edge of the shoal, and upon the best of the flood to thrust over, which shoal *John Douglas* buoyed and beckoned[69] for them before. But they laboured in vain; for neither could they turn it up altogether so far to the east, neither did the flood continue so long, but the water fell ere they could have passed the sands, as we after found by a second experience. So as now we must either give over our enterprise, or, leaving our ships at adventure 400 miles behind us, to run up in our ship's boats, one barge, and two wherries. But being doubtful how to carry victuals for so long a time in such baubles, or any strength of men, especially for that *Berreo* assured us that his son must be by that time come down with many soldiers, I sent away one *King*, master of the *Lion's Whelp*, with his ship's boat, to try another branch of a river in the bottom of the bay of *Guanipa*, which was called *Amana*, to prove if there were water to be found for either of the small ships to enter. But when he came to the mouth of *Amana*, he found it as the rest, but stayed not to discover it thoroughly, because he was assured by an Indian, his guide, that the cannibals of *Guanipa* would assail them with many *canoas*, and that they shot poisoned arrows; so as if he hasted not back, they should all be lost.

In the meantime, fearing the worst, I caused all the carpenters we had to cut down a *gallego* boat, which we meant to cast off, and to fit her with banks to row on, and in all things to prepare her the best they could, so as she might be brought to draw but five foot, for so much we had on the bar of *Capuri* at low water. And doubting of *King's* return, I sent *John Douglas* again in my long barge, as well to relieve him as also to make a perfect search in the bottom of the bay. For it hath been held for infallible that whatsoever ship or boat shall fall therein can never disemboque again, by reason of the violent current which setteth into the said bay, as also for that the breeze and easterly wind bloweth directly into the same. Of which opinion I have

---

[69] Marked or furnished with beacons.

heard *John Hampton* of *Plymouth*,[70] one of the greatest experience of *England*, and divers other besides that have traded [to] *Trinidad*.

I sent with *John Douglas* an old *cacique* of *Trinidad* for a pilot, who told us that we could not return again by the bay or gulf, but that he knew a by-branch which ran within the land to the eastward, and that he thought by it we might fall into *Capuri*, and so return in four days. *John Douglas* searched those rivers, and found four goodly entrances, whereof the least was as big as the *Thames* at *Woolwich*, but in the bay thitherward it was shoal and but six foot water; so as we were now without hope of any ship or bark to pass over, and therefore resolved to go on with the boats, and the bottom of the *gallego*, in which we thrust 60 men. In the *Lion's Whelp's* boat and wherry we carried twenty, Captain *Caulfield* in his wherry carried ten more, and in my barge other ten, which made up a hundred; we had no other means but to carry victual for a month in the same, and also to lodge therein as we could, and to boil and dress our meat. Captain *Gifford* had with him Master *Edward Porter*, Captain *Eynos*, and eight more in his wherry, with all their victual, weapons, and provisions. Captain *Caulfield* had with him my cousin *Butshead Gorges* and eight more. In the galley, of gentlemen and officers myself had Captain *Thyn*, my cousin *John Grenville*, my nephew *John Gilbert*, Captain *Whiddon*, Captain *Keymis*, *Edward Hancock*, Captain *Clarke*, Lieutenant *Hughes*, *Thomas Upton*, Captain *Facy*, *Jerome Ferrar*, *Anthony Wells*, *William Connock*, and about fifty more. We could not learn of *Berreo* any other way to enter but in branches, so far to the windward as it was impossible for us to recover; for we had as much sea to cross over in our wherries as between *Dover* and *Callys*,[71] and in a great billow, the wind and current being both very strong. So as we were driven to go in those small boats directly before the wind into the bottom of the bay of *Guanipa*, and from thence to enter the mouth of some one of those rivers which *John Douglas* had last discovered; and had with us for pilot an Indian of *Barema*, a river to the south of *Orenoque*, between that and *Amazones*, whose *canoas* we had formerly taken as he was going from the said *Barema*, laden with *cassavi* bread to sell at *Margarita*. This *Arwacan* promised to bring me into the great river of *Orenoque*; but indeed of that which we entered he was utterly ignorant, for he had not seen

---

[70]Hampton was captain of the *Minion*, which formed part of Hawkins's third voyage across the Atlantic in 1567.

[71]The crossing from Dover, England, to Calais, France, is just over twenty miles.

it in twelve years before, at which time he was very young, and of no judgment. And if God had not sent us another help, we might have wandered a whole year in that labyrinth of rivers, ere we had found any way, either out or in, especially after we were past the ebbing and flowing, which was in four days. For I know all the earth doth not yield the like confluence of streams and branches, the one crossing the other so many times, and all so fair and large, and so like one to another, as no man can tell which to take. And if we went by the sun or compass, hoping thereby to go directly one way or other, yet that way we were also carried in a circle amongst multitudes of islands, and every island so bordered with high trees, as no man could see any further than the breadth of the river, or length of the breach. But this it chanced, that entering into a river (which because it had no name, we called the *River of the Red Cross*, ourselves being the first Christians that ever came therein),[72] the 22 of May, as we were rowing up the same, we espied a small *canoa* with three Indians, which, by the swiftness of my barge, rowing with eight oars, I overtook ere they could cross the river. The rest of the people on the banks, shadowed under the thick wood, gazed on with a doubtful conceit what might befall those three which we had taken. But when they perceived that we offered them no violence, neither entered their *canoa* with any of ours, nor took out of the *canoa* any of theirs, they then began to show themselves on the bank's side, and offered to traffic with us for such things as they had. And as we drew near, they all stayed; and we came with our barge to the mouth of a little creek which came from their town into the great river.

As we abode there a while, our Indian pilot, called *Ferdinando*, would needs go ashore to their village to fetch some fruits and to drink of their artificial[73] wines, and also to see the place and to know the lord of it against another time, and took with him a brother of his which he had with him in the journey. When they came to the village of these people, the lord of the island offered to lay hands on them, purposing to have slain them both, yielding for reason that this Indian of ours had brought a strange nation into their territory to spoil and destroy them. But the pilot being quick and of a disposed body, slipped their

---

[72]Ralegh gives this river—which had been visited before by Spaniards—a name pregnant with meaning, alluding as it does to the emblem of Saint George, patron saint of England (an emblem still featured on the Union Jack), and to the "Knight of the Red Crosse," the hero of book 1 of Spenser's *Faerie Queene*.

[73]Skillfully made.

fingers and ran into the woods, and his brother, being the better foot-man of the two, recovered the creek's mouth, where we stayed in our barge, crying out that his brother was slain. With that we set hands on one of them that was next us, a very old man, and brought him into the barge, assuring him that if we had not our pilot again we would presently cut off his head. This old man, being resolved that he should pay the loss of the other, cried out to those in the woods to save *Ferdinando* our pilot; but they followed him notwithstanding, and hunted after him upon the foot with their deer-dogs, and with so many a cry that all the woods echoed with the shout they made. But at the last this poor chased Indian recovered the river side and got upon a tree, and, as we were coasting, leaped down and swam to the barge half dead with fear. But our good hap was that we kept the other old Indian, which we handfasted[74] to redeem our pilot withal; for, being natural of those rivers, we assured ourselves that he knew the way better than any stranger could. And, indeed, but for this chance, I think we had never found the way either to *Guiana* or back to our ships; for *Ferdinando* after a few days knew nothing at all, nor which way to turn; yea, and many times the old man himself was in great doubt which river to take. Those people which dwell in these broken islands and drowned lands are generally called *Tivitivas*. There are of them two sorts, the one called *Ciawani*, and the other *Waraweete*.

The great river of *Orenoque* or *Baraquan* hath nine branches which fall out on the north side of his own main mouth. On the south side it hath seven other fallings into the sea, so it disemboqueth[75] by sixteen arms in all, between islands and broken ground; but the islands are very great, many of them as big as the *Isle of Wight* and bigger, and many less. From the first branch on the north to the last of the south it is at least 100 leagues, so as the river's mouth is no less than 300 miles wide at his entrance into the sea, which I take to be far bigger than that of *Amazones*. All those that inhabit in the mouth of this river upon the several north branches are these *Tivitivas*, of which there are two chief lords which have continual wars one with the other. The islands which lie on the right hand are called *Pallamos*, and the land on the left *Hororotomaka*; and the river by which *John Douglas* returned within the land from *Amana* to *Capuri* they call *Macuri*.

These *Tivitivas* are a very goodly people and very valiant, and have the most manly speech and most deliberate that ever I heard of what

---

[74]Seized; fastened the hands of.
[75]Discharges itself.

nation soever. In the summer they have houses on the ground, as in other places. In the winter they dwell upon the trees, where they build very artificial[76] towns and villages,[77] as it is written in the Spanish story of the *West Indies* that those people do in the low lands near the gulf of *Uraba*. For between May and September the river of *Orenoque* riseth thirty foot upright, and then are those islands overflown twenty foot high above the level of the ground, saving some few raised grounds in the middle of them; and for this cause they are enforced to live in this manner. They never eát of anything that is set or sown; and as at home they use neither planting nor other manurance,[78] so when they come abroad they refuse to feed of aught but of that which nature without labour bringeth forth. They use the tops of *palmitos*[79] for bread, and kill deer, fish, and porks for the rest of their sustenance. They have also many sorts of fruits that grow in the woods, and great variety of birds and fowls.

And if to speak of them were not tedious and vulgar, surely we saw in those passages of very rare colours and forms not elsewhere to be found, for as much as I have either seen or read. Of these people those that dwell upon the branches of *Orenoque*, called *Capuri* and *Macureo*, are for the most part carpenters of *canoas*; for they make the most and fairest houses [*canoas*], and sell them into *Guiana* for gold and into *Trinidad* for Tobacco, in the excessive taking whereof they exceed all nations. And notwithstanding the moistness of the air in which they live, the hardness of their diet, and the great labours they suffer to hunt, fish, and fowl for their living, in all my life, either in the *Indies* or in *Europe*, did I never behold a more goodly or better-favoured people, or a more manly. They were wont to make war upon all nations, and especially on the *Cannibals*, so as none durst without a good strength trade by those rivers; but of late they are at peace with their neighbours, all holding the Spaniards for a common enemy. When their commanders die, they use great lamentation; and when they think the flesh of their bodies is putrified and fallen from their

---

[76]Skillfully made or constructed; displaying technical skill. Ralegh's use of this term here, as in other passages (see note 73), invokes a Renaissance debate on culture and the apposition of "art" and "nature." By admiring the ingenuity and "artifice" of the Tivitivas ("a very goodly people"), Ralegh is also implying their possession of civility — making them suitable allies of the English.

[77]See Document 3, Figure 7.

[78]Cultivation of land; tillage. (Later: manuring; fertilizing.)

[79]*Palmito* (palmetto) is a relatively generic term for the ite or ita palm (*Mauritia flexuosa*), which was consumed as a staple, in contrast to cassava (manioc) or maize.

bones, then they take up the carcass again and hang it in the *cacique's* house that died, and deck his skull with feathers of all colours, and hang all his gold plates about the bones of his arms, thighs, and legs. Those nations which are called *Arwacas*, which dwell on the south of *Orenoque* (of which place and nation our Indian pilot was), are dispersed in many other places, and do use to beat the bones of their lords into powder, and their wives and friends drink it all in their several sorts of drinks.[80]

After we departed from the port of these *Ciawani*, we passed up the river with the flood and anchored the ebb, and in this sort we went onward. The third day that we entered the river our galley came on ground and stuck so fast as we thought that even there our discovery had ended, and that we must have left 60 of our men to have inhabited, like rooks upon trees, with those nations. But the next morning, after we had cast out all her ballast, with tugging and hauling to and fro, we got her afloat and went on. At four days' end we fell into as goodly a river as ever I beheld, which was called the great *Amana*, which ran more directly without windings and turnings than the other. But soon after the flood of the sea left us, and we [being] enforced either by main strength to row against a violent current, or to return as wise as[81] we went out, we had then no shift[82] but to persuade the companies that it was but two or three days' work, and therefore desired them to take pains, every gentleman and other taking their turns to row, and to spell one the other at the hour's end. Every day we passed by goodly branches of rivers, some falling from the west, others from the east, into *Amana*; but those I leave to the description in the chart of discovery, where every one shall be named with his rising and descent. When three days more were overgone, our companies began to despair, the weather being extreme hot, the river bordered with very high trees that kept away the air, and the current against us every day stronger than other. But we evermore commanded our pilots to promise an end the next day, and used it so long as we were driven to assure them from four reaches of the river to three, and so to two, and so to the next reach. But so long we laboured as many days were spent, and so driven to draw ourselves to harder allowance, our bread even at the last, and no drink at all; and

---

[80]Whitehead validates many of Ralegh's proto-ethnographic observations, including these comments on indigenous funerary customs.

[81]The way that.

[82]Available means of effecting an end.

our men and ourselves so wearied and scorched, and doubtful withal whether we should ever perform it or no, the heat increasing as we drew towards the line; for we were now in five degrees.[83]

The further we went on (our victual decreasing and the air breeding great faintness) we grew weaker and weaker, when we had most need of strength and ability. For hourly the river ran more violently than other against us, and the barge, wherries, and ship's boat of Captain *Gifford* and Captain *Caulfield* had spent all their provisions; so as we were brought into despair and discomfort, had we not persuaded all the company that it was but only one day's work more to attain the land where we should be relieved of all we wanted, and if we returned, that we were sure to starve by the way, and that the world would also laugh us to scorn. On the banks of these rivers were divers sorts of fruits good to eat, flowers and trees of that variety as were sufficient to make ten volumes of herbals;[84] we relieved ourselves many times with the fruits of the country, and sometimes with fowl and fish. We saw birds of all colours, some carnation, some crimson, orange-tawny, purple, green, watchet,[85] and of all other sorts, both simple and mixed, as it was unto us a great good passing of the time to behold them, besides the relief we found by killing some store of them with our fowling-pieces;[86] without which, having little or no bread, and less drink, but only the thick and troubled water of the river, we had been in a very hard case.

Our old pilot of the *Ciawani* (whom, as I said before, we took to redeem *Ferdinando*) told us that, if we would enter a branch of a river on the right hand with our barge and wherries, and leave the galley at anchor the while in the great river, he would bring us to a town of the *Arwacas*, where we should find store of bread, hens, fish, and of the country wine; and persuaded us that departing from the galley at noon, we might return ere night. I was very glad to hear this speech, and presently took my barge, with eight musketeers, Captain *Gifford's* wherry, with himself and four musketeers, and Captain *Caulfield* with his wherry and as many, and so we entered the mouth of this river; and because we were persuaded that it was so near, we took no victual with us at all. When we had rowed three hours, we marvelled we saw no sign of any dwelling, and asked the pilot where the town was; he

[83]Ralegh is off. His men would have been about 9° north of the equator (hot though it certainly would have been).
[84]Books on the exotic flora.
[85]Light blue or sky blue.
[86]Guns; specifically, guns used to shoot birds.

told us a little further. After three hours more, the sun being almost set, we began to suspect that he led us that way to betray us; for he confessed that those Spaniards which fled from *Trinidad*, and also those that remained with *Carapana* in *Emeria*, were joined together in some village upon that river. But when it grew towards night, and we demanded where the place was, he told us but four reaches more. When we had rowed four and four, we saw no sign; and our poor watermen, even heart-broken and tired, were ready to give up the ghost; for we had now come from the galley near forty miles.

At the last we determined to hang the pilot; and if we had well known the way back again by night, he had surely gone. But our own necessities pleaded sufficiently for his safety; for it was as dark as pitch, and the river began so to narrow itself, and the trees to hang over from side to side, as we were driven with arming swords to cut a passage through those branches that covered the water. We were very desirous to find this town hoping of a feast, because we made but a short breakfast aboard the galley in the morning, and it was now eight o'clock at night, and our stomachs began to gnaw apace; but whether it was best to return or go on, we began to doubt, suspecting treason in the pilot more and more. But the poor old Indian ever assured us that it was but a little further, but this one turning and that turning; and at last about one o'clock after midnight we saw a light, and rowing towards it we heard the dogs of the village. When we landed we found few people; for the lord of that place was gone with divers *canoas* above 400 miles off, upon a journey towards the head of *Orenoque*, to trade for gold, and to buy women of the *Cannibals*, who afterwards unfortunately passed by us as we rode at an anchor in the port of *Morequito* in the dark of the night, and yet came so near us as his *canoas* grated against our barges; he left one of his company at the port of *Morequito*, by whom we understood that he had brought thirty young women, divers plates of gold, and had great store of fine pieces of cotton cloth and cotton beds. In his house we had good store of bread, fish, hens, and Indian drink, and so rested that night; and in the morning, after we had traded with such of his people as came down, we returned towards our galley, and brought with us some quantity of bread, fish, and hens.

On both sides of this river, we passed the most beautiful country that ever mine eyes beheld; and whereas all that we had seen before was nothing but woods, prickles, bushes, and thorns, here we beheld plains of twenty miles in length, the grass short and green, and in divers parts groves of trees by themselves, as if they had been by all

the art and labour in the world so made of purpose; and still as we
rowed, the deer came down feeding by the water's side, as if they had
been used to a keeper's call. Upon this river there were great store of
fowl, and of many sorts; we saw in it divers sorts of strange fishes, and
of marvellous bigness; but for *lagartos*[87] it exceeded, for there were
thousands of those ugly serpents; and the people call it, for the abundance of them, the *River of Lagartos*, in their language. I had a Negro,
a very proper young fellow, that leaping out of the galley to swim in
the mouth of this river, was in all our sights taken and devoured with
one of those *lagartos*. In the meanwhile our companies in the galley
thought we had been all lost (for we promised to return before night)
and sent the *Lion's Whelp's* ship's boat with Captain *Whiddon* to follow
us up the river. But the next day, after we had rowed up and down
some four score miles, we returned, and went on our way up the great
river; and when we were even at the last cast for want of victuals, Captain *Gifford* being before the galley and the rest of the boats, seeking
out some place to land upon the banks to make fire, espied four
canoas coming down the river, and with no small joy caused his men
to try the uttermost of their strengths; and after a while, two of the
four gave over and ran themselves ashore, every man betaking himself to the fastness of the woods. The two other lesser got away, while
he landed to lay hold on these; and so turned into some by-creek, we
knew not whither. Those *canoas* that were taken were loaden with
bread, and were bound for *Margarita* in the *West Indies*, which those
Indians (called *Arwacas*) proposed to carry thither for exchange. But
in the lesser there were three Spaniards, who, having heard of the
defeat of their Governor in *Trinidad*, and that we purposed to enter
Guiana, came away in those *canoas*; one of them was a *Cavallero*[88] as
the captain of the *Arwacas* after told us, another a soldier, and the
third a refiner.

   In the meantime, nothing on the earth could have been more welcome to us, next unto gold, than the great store of very excellent
bread which we found in these *canoas*; for now our men cried, *Let us*

[87]Literally, in Spanish, "lizards." Anglicized as "alligators," denoting a species of
South American caiman.
   [88]Cavalier: a horseman or horse soldier. Identified as Captain Phelipe de Santiago,
who first served Berrio but later deserted him for Francisco de Vides. This and many
other references that Ralegh makes to Spanish actions in the region can be confirmed
by Spanish archival documents, many recorded in Harlow. See Sir Walter Ralegh, *The
Discoverie of the Large and Bewtiful Empire of Guiana*, ed. V. T. Harlow (London: Argonaut Press, 1928).

go on, we care not how far. After that Captain *Gifford* had brought the two *canoas* to the galley, I took my barge and went to the bank's side with a dozen shot, where the *canoas* first ran themselves ashore, and landed there, sending out Captain *Gifford* and Captain *Thyn* on the one hand, and Captain *Caulfield* on the other, to follow those that were fled into the woods. And as I was creeping through the bushes, I saw an Indian basket hidden, which was the refiner's basket; for I found in it his quicksilver, saltpeter, and divers things for the trial of metals, and also the dust of such ore as he had refined; but in those *canoas* which escaped there was a good quantity of ore and gold.[89] I then landed more men, and offered five hundred pound to what soldier soever could take one of those three Spaniards that we thought were landed. But our labours were in vain in that behalf, for they put themselves into one of the small *canoas*, and so, while the greater *canoas* were in taking, they escaped. But seeking after the Spaniards, we found the *Arwacas* hidden in the woods, which were pilots for the Spaniards, and rowed their *canoas*. Of which I kept the chiefest for a pilot, and carried him with me to *Guiana*; by whom I understood where and in what countries the Spaniards had laboured for gold, though I made not the same known to all. For when the springs began to break, and the rivers to raise themselves so suddenly as by no means we could abide the digging of any mine, especially for that the richest are defended with rocks of hard stones, which we call the *white spar*, and that it required both time, men, and instruments fit for such a work, I thought it best not to hover thereabouts, lest if the same had been perceived by the company, there would have been by this time many barks and ships set out, and perchance other nations would also have gotten of ours for pilots; so as both ourselves might have been prevented, and all our care taken for good usage of the people been utterly lost, by those that only respect present profit; and such violence or insolence offered as the nations which are borderers would have changed their desire of our love and defence into hatred and violence. And for any longer stay to have brought a more quantity (which I hear hath been often objected) whosoever had seen or proved the fury of that river after it began to arise, and had been a month and odd days, as we were, from hearing aught from our ships, leaving them meanly manned above 400 miles off, would perchance have turned

---

[89]This is necessarily conjecture and also typical of Ralegh's narrative of near misses (several examples of which follow in this paragraph). He is perpetually thwarted and unlucky, if valiant and noble in his efforts.

somewhat sooner than we did, if all the mountains had been gold, or rich stones. And to say the truth, all the branches and small rivers which fell into *Orenoque* were raised with such speed, as if we waded them over the shoes in the morning outward, we were covered to the shoulders homeward the very same day; and to stay to dig out gold with our nails, had been *opus laboris* but not *ingenii.*[90] Such a quantity as would have served our turns we could not have had, but a discovery of the mines to our infinite disadvantage we had made, and that could have been the best profit of farther search or stay; for those mines are not easily broken, nor opened in haste, and I could have returned a good quantity of gold ready cast, if I had not shot at another mark than present profit.

This *Arwacan* pilot, with the rest, feared that we would have eaten them, or otherwise have put them to some cruel death; for the Spaniards, to the end that none of the people in the passage towards *Guiana*, or in *Guiana* itself, might come to speech with us, persuaded all the nations that we were men-eaters and cannibals. But when the poor men and women had seen us, and that we gave them meat, and to every one something or other which was rare and strange to them, they began to conceive the deceit and purpose of the Spaniards, who indeed (as they confessed) took from them both their wives and daughters daily, and used them for the satisfying of their own lusts, especially such as they took in this manner by strength. But I protest before the Majesty of the living God, that I neither know nor believe that any of our company one or other, by violence or otherwise, ever knew[91] any of their women, and yet we saw many hundreds, and had many in our power, and of those very young and excellently favoured, which came among us without deceit, stark naked. Nothing got us more love amongst them than this usage; for I suffered not any man to take from any of the nations so much as a *pina*[92] or a *potato* root without giving them contentment, nor any man so much as to offer to touch any of their wives or daughters; which course, so contrary to the Spaniards (who tyrannize over them in all things), drew them to admire her Majesty, whose commandment I told them it was, and also wonderfully to honour our nation. But I confess it was a very impatient work to keep the meaner sort from spoil and stealing when we came to their houses; which because in all I could not prevent, I

[90] Laborious work, but not smart (ingenious or clever) to undertake.
[91] Had sexual relations with.
[92] Pineapple.

caused my Indian interpreter at every place when we departed to know of the loss or wrong done, and if aught were stolen or taken by violence, either the same was restored and the party punished in their sight, or else was paid for to their uttermost demand. They also much wondered at us, after they heard that we had slain the Spaniards at *Trinidad*, for they were before resolved that no nation of *Christians* durst abide their presence; and they wondered more when I had made them know of the great overthrow that her Majesty's army and fleet had given them of late years in their own countries.

After we had taken in this supply of bread, with divers baskets of roots, which were excellent meat, I gave one of the *canoas* to the *Arwacas*, which belonged to the Spaniards that were escaped; and when I had dismissed all but the captain (who by the Spaniards was christened *Martin*), I sent back in the same *canoa* the old *Ciawan* and *Ferdinando*, my first pilot, and gave them both such things as they desired, with sufficient victual to carry them back, and by them wrote a letter to the ships, which they promised to deliver, and performed it; and then I went on with my new hired pilot, *Martin* the *Arwacan*. But the next or second day after, we came aground again with our galley, and were like to cast her away, with all our victual and provision, and so lay on the sand one whole night, and were far more in despair at this time to free her than before, because we had no tide of flood to help us, and therefore feared that all our hopes would have ended in mishaps. But we fastened an anchor upon the land, and with main strength drew her off; and so the fifteenth day we discovered afar off the mountains of *Guiana*[93] to our great joy, and towards the evening had a slent[94] of a northerly wind that blew very strong, which brought us in sight of the great river *Orenoque*, out of which this river descended wherein we were. We descried afar off three other *canoas* as far as we could discern them, after whom we hastened with our barge and wherries, but two of them passed out of sight, and the third entered up the great river, on the right hand to the westward, and there stayed out of sight, thinking that we meant to take the way eastward towards the province of *Carapana*; for that way the Spaniards keep, not daring to go upwards to *Guiana*, the people in those parts being all their enemies, and those in the *canoas* thought us to have been those Spaniards that were fled from *Trinidad* and had escaped killing. And when we came so far down as the opening of that branch

---

[93] This is likely the Serranía (or Sierra) de Imataca.
[94] Slight breeze or spell of wind.

into which they slipped, being near them with our barge and wherries, we made after them, and ere they could land came within call, and by our interpreter told them what we were, wherewith they came back willingly aboard us; and of such fish and *tortugas'* eggs[95] as they had gathered they gave us, and promised in the morning to bring the lord of that part with them, and to do us all other services they could. That night we came to an anchor at the parting of three goodly rivers (the one was the river of *Amana*, by which we came from the north and ran athwart towards the south; the other two were of *Orenoque*, which crossed from the west and ran to the sea towards the east)[96] and landed upon a fair sand, where we found thousands of *tortugas'* eggs, which are very wholesome meat and greatly restoring; so as our men were now well filled and highly contented both with the fare and nearness of the land of *Guiana*, which appeared in sight.

In the morning there came down, according to promise, the lord of that border, called *Toparimaca*, with some thirty or forty followers, and brought us divers sorts of fruits, and of his wine, bread, fish, and flesh, whom we also feasted as we could; at least he drank good Spanish wine (whereof we had a small quantity in bottles) which above all things they love. I conferred with this *Toparimaca* of the next[97] way to *Guiana*, who conducted our galley and boats to his own port, and carried us from thence some mile and a half to his town, where some of our captains garoused[98] of his wine till they were reasonable pleasant, for it is very strong with pepper, and the juice of divers herbs and fruits digested and purged. They keep it in great earthen pots of ten or twelve gallons, very clean and sweet, and are themselves at their meetings and feasts the greatest garousers and drunkards of the world. When we came to his town we found two *caciques*, whereof one was a stranger that had been up the river in trade, and his boats, people, and wife encamped at the port where we anchored; and the other was of that country, a follower of *Toparimaca*. They lay each of them in a cotton *hamaca*, which we call brazil beds, and two women attending them with six cups and a little ladle to fill them out of an earthen pitcher of wine; and so they drank each of them three of those cups at a time, one to the other, and in this sort they drink drunk at their feasts and meetings.

---

[95] Freshwater turtles' eggs, at that time plentiful on the river's sandbars.

[96] This would have been the junction of Ralegh's "River of the Red Cross" (now known as the Caño Manamo) and the Orinoco. Ralegh anchored not far from the modern town of Barrancas.

[97] Nearest—that is, best.

[98] Caroused: drank freely.

That *cacique* that was a stranger had his wife staying at the port where we anchored, and in all my life I have seldom seen a better favoured woman. She was of good stature, with black eyes, fat of body, of an excellent countenance, her hair almost as long as herself, tied up again in pretty knots; and it seemed she stood not in that awe of her husband as the rest, for she spake and discoursed, and drank among the gentlemen and captains, and was very pleasant, knowing her own comeliness, and taking great pride therein. I have seen a lady in *England* so like to her, as but for the difference of colour, I would have sworn might have been the same.

The seat of this town of *Toparimaca* was very pleasant, standing on a little hill, in an excellent prospect, with goodly gardens a mile compass round about it, and two very fair and large ponds of excellent fish adjoining. This town is called *Arowacai*; the people are of the nation called *Nepoios*, and are followers of *Carapana*. In that place I saw very aged people, that we might perceive all their sinews and veins without any flesh, and but even as a case covered only with skin. The lord of this place gave me an old man for pilot, who was of great experience and travel, and knew the river most perfectly both by day and night. And it shall be requisite for any man that passeth it to have such a pilot; for it is four, five, and six miles over in many places, and twenty miles in other places, with wonderful eddies and strong currents, many great islands and divers shoals, and many dangerous rocks; and besides upon any increase of wind so great a billow, as we were sometimes in great peril of drowning in the galley, for the small boats durst not come from the shore but when it was very fair.

The next day we hastened thence, and having an easterly wind to help us, we spared our arms from rowing; for after we entered *Orenoque*, the river lieth for the most part east and west, even from the sea unto *Quito*, in *Peru*.[99] This river is navigable with ships little less than 1,000 miles; and from the place where we entered it may be sailed up in small pinnaces to many of the best parts of *Nuevo Reyno de Granada* and of *Popayan*. And from no place may the cities of these parts of the *Indies* be so easily taken and invaded as from hence. All that day we sailed up a branch of that river, having on the left hand a great island, which they call *Assapana*,[100] which may contain some

---

[99]This is way off in terms of latitude, but it suggests, first, Ralegh's deft conflation of his "discoveries" with his Spanish predecessors' (in this case, Berrio's descent from Bogotá, which lies considerably closer in latitude to Quito) and, second, his rhetorical effort to affiliate the geography he explored in the east with the great stores of precious metals known to exist in the west.

[100]Island of Yaya.

five-and-twenty miles in length and six miles in breadth, the great body of the river running on the other side of this island. Beyond that middle branch there is also another island in the river, called *Iwana*,[101] which is twice as big as the Isle of *Wight*; and beyond it, and between it and the main of *Guiana*, runneth a third branch of *Orenoque*, called *Arraroopana*. All three are goodly branches, and all navigable for great ships. I judge the river in this place to be at least thirty miles broad, reckoning the islands which divide the branches in it, for afterwards I sought also both the other branches.

After we reached to the head of this island called *Assapana*, a little to the westward on the right hand there opened a river which came from the north, called *Europa*,[102] and fell into the great river; and beyond it on the same side we anchored for that night by another island, six miles long and two miles broad, which they call *Ocaywita*. From hence, in the morning, we landed two *Guianians*, which we found in the town of *Toparimaca*, that came with us; who went to give notice of our coming to the lord of that country, called *Putyma*, a follower of *Topiawari*, chief lord of *Aromaia*, who succeeded *Morequito*, whom (as you have heard before) *Berreo* put to death. But his town being far within the land, he came not unto us that day; so as we anchored again that night near the banks of another island, of bigness much like the other, which they call *Putapayma*; on the main land, over against which island was a very high mountain called *Oecope*. We coveted to anchor rather by these islands in the river than by the main, because of the *tortugas'* eggs, which our people found on them in great abundance; and also because the ground served better for us to cast our nets for fish, the main banks being for the most part stony and high, and the rocks of a blue, metalline colour, like unto the best steel ore, which I assuredly take it to be. Of the same blue stone are also divers great mountains, which border this river in many places.

The next morning towards nine of the clock, we weighed anchor; and the breeze increasing, we sailed always west up the river, and, after a while, opening the land on the right side, the country appeared to be champaign,[103] and the banks shewed very perfect red. I therefore sent two of the little barges with Captain *Gifford*, and with him Captain *Thyn*, Captain *Caulfield*, my cousin *Grenville*, my nephew *John Gilbert*, Captain *Eynos*, Master *Edward Porter*, and my cousin *Butshead*

---

[101] Island of Tortola.
[102] Guaraguapo River.
[103] Flat, level, and open.

Gorges, with some few soldiers, to march over the banks of that red land and to discover what manner of country it was on the other side; who at their return found it all a plain level as far as they went or could discern from the highest tree they could get upon. And my old pilot, a man of great travel, brother to the *cacique Toparimaca*, told me that those were called the plains of the *Sayma*, and that the same level reached to *Cumaná* and *Caracas*, in the *West Indies*, which are a hundred and twenty leagues to the north, and that there inhabited four principal nations. The first were the *Sayma*, the next *Assawai*, the third and greatest the *Wikiri* (by whom *Pedro Hernandez de Serpa*, before mentioned, was overthrown as he passed with 300 horses from *Cumaná* towards *Orenoque* in his enterprise of *Guiana*). The fourth are called *Aroras*, and are as black as Negroes, but have smooth hair;[104] and these are very valiant, or rather desperate, people, and have the most strong poison on their arrows, and most dangerous of all nations, of which I will speak somewhat, being a digression not unnecessary.

There was nothing whereof I was more curious than to find out the true remedies of these poisoned arrows. For besides the mortality of the wound they make, the party shot endureth the most insufferable torment in the world, and abideth a most ugly and lamentable death, sometimes dying stark mad, sometimes their bowels breaking out of their bellies, [which] are presently discoloured as black as pitch, and so unsavory as no man can endure to cure or to attend them. And it is more strange to know that in all this time there was never Spaniard, either by gift or torment, that could attain to the true knowledge of the cure, although they have martyred and put to invented torture I know not how many of them. But every one of these Indians know it not, no, not one among thousands, but their soothsayers and priests, who do conceal it, and only teach it but from the father to the son.

Those medicines which are vulgar, and serve for the ordinary poison, are made of the juice of a root called *tupara*;[105] the same also quencheth marvellously the heat of burning fevers, and healeth inward wounds and broken veins that bleed within the body. But I was more beholden to the *Guianians* than any other; for *Antonio de Berreo* told

---

[104]These may be identified with the Chayma, Assawanú, Guayqueri, and Yaruro peoples. The Yaruro ("Aroras") were "black as Negroes" owing to their use of body paint.

[105]Identified as curare or *ourari*. The more complex, powerful poisons noted in the previous passage were mentioned by other travelers as well.

me that he could never attain to the knowledge thereof, and yet they taught me the best way of healing as well thereof as of all other poisons. Some of the Spaniards have been cured in ordinary wounds of the common poisoned arrows with the juice of garlic. But this is a general rule for all men that shall hereafter travel the *Indies* where poisoned arrows are used, that they must abstain from drink. For if they take any liquor into their body, as they shall be marvellously provoked thereunto by drought,[106] I say, if they drink before the wound be dressed, or soon upon it, there is no way with them but present death.

And so I will return again to our journey, which for this third day we finished, and cast anchor again near the continent on the left hand between two mountains, the one called *Aroami* and the other *Aio*. I made no stay here but till midnight; for I feared hourly lest any rain should fall, and then it had been impossible to have gone any further up, notwithstanding that there is every day a very strong breeze and easterly wind. I deferred the search of the country on *Guiana* side till my return down the river.

The next day we sailed by a great island in the middle of the river, called *Manoripano*; and, as we walked a while on the island, while the galley got ahead of us, there came for us from the main a small *canoa* with seven or eight *Guianians*, to invite us to anchor at their port, but I deferred till my return. It was that *cacique* to whom those *Nepoios* went, which came with us from the town of *Toparimaca*. And so the fifth day we reached as high up as the province of *Aromaia*, the country of *Morequito*, whom *Berreo* executed, and anchored to the west of an island called *Murrecotima*, ten miles long and five broad. And that night the cacique *Aramiary*, to whose town we made our long and hungry voyage out of the river of *Amana*, passed by us.

The next day we arrived at the port of *Morequito* and anchored there, sending away one of our pilots to seek the king of *Aromaia*, uncle to *Morequito*, slain by *Berreo* as aforesaid. The next day following, before noon, he came to us on foot from his house, which was fourteen English miles (himself being 110 years old), and returned on foot the same day; and with him many of the borderers, with many women and children, that came to wonder at our nation and to bring us down victual, which they did in great plenty, as venison, pork, hens, chickens, fowl, fish, with divers sorts of excellent fruits and roots, and great abundance of *pinas*, the princess of fruits that grow under the

---

[106]Dryness or thirst.

sun, especially those of *Guiana*. They brought us, also, store of bread and of their wine, and a sort of *paraquitos*[107] no bigger than wrens, and of all other sorts both small and great. One of them gave me a beast called by the Spaniards *armadillo*, which they call *cassacam*, which seemeth to be all barred over with small plates somewhat like to a *Rhinoceros*, with a white horn growing in his hinder parts as big as a great hunting-horn, which they use to wind[108] instead of a trumpet. *Monardus* writeth that a little of the powder of that horn put into the ear cureth deafness.[109]

After this old king had rested a while in a little tent that I caused to be set up, I began by my interpreter to discourse with him of the death of *Morequito*, his predecessor, and afterward of the Spaniards; and ere I went any farther I made him know the cause of my coming thither, whose servant I was, and that the Queen's pleasure was I should undertake the voyage for their defence and to deliver them from the tyranny of the Spaniards, dilating at large (as I had done before to those of *Trinidad*) her Majesty's greatness, her justice, her charity to all oppressed nations, with as many of the rest of her beauties and virtues as either I could express or they conceive. All which being with great admiration attentively heard and marvellously admired, I began to sound [out] the old man as touching *Guiana* and the state thereof, what sort of commonwealth it was, how governed, of what strength and policy, how far it extended, and what nations were friends or enemies adjoining, and finally of the distance and way to enter the same. He told me that himself and his people, with all those down the river towards the sea, as far as *Emeria*, the province of *Carapana*, were of *Guiana*, but that they called themselves *Orenoqueponi*, because they bordered the great river *Orenoque*; and that all the nations between the river and those mountains in sight, called *Wacarima*, were of the same cast and appellation; and that on the other side of those mountains of *Wacarima* there was a large plain (which after I discovered in my return) called the valley of *Amariocapana*. In all that valley the people were also of the ancient *Guianians*.

I asked what nations those were which inhabited on the further side of those mountains, beyond the valley of *Amariocapana*. He

---

[107] Parakeets.

[108] Blow.

[109] Nicolás Monardes's history of Indian medicine, the *Historia Medicinal* (Seville, 1574), was translated into English in 1577.

answered with a great sigh (as a man which had inward feeling of the loss of his country and liberty, especially for that his eldest son was slain in a battle on that side of the mountains, whom he most entirely loved) that he remembered in his father's lifetime, when he was very old and himself a young man, that there came down into that large valley of *Guiana* a nation from so far off as the sun slept (for such were his own words), with so great a multitude as they could not be numbered nor resisted, and that they wore large coats, and hats of crimson colour, which colour he expressed by shewing a piece of red wood wherewith my tent was supported, and that they were called *Orejones* and *Epuremei*; those that had slain and rooted out so many of the ancient people as there were leaves in the wood upon all the trees, and had now made themselves lords of all, even to that mountain foot called *Curaa*, saving only of two nations, the one called *Iwarawaqueri* and the other *Cassipagotos*; and that, in the last battle fought between the *Epuremei* and the *Iwarawaqueri*, his eldest son was chosen to carry to the aid of the *Iwarawaqueri* a great troop of the *Orenoqueponi*, and was there slain with all his people and friends, and that he had now remaining but one son; and farther told me that those *Epuremei* had built a great town called *Macureguarai* at the said mountain foot, at the beginning of the great plains of *Guiana*, which have no end; and that their houses have many rooms, one over the other, and that therein the great king of the *Orejones* and *Epuremei* kept three thousand men to defend the borders against them, and withal daily to invade and slay them; but that of late years, since the Christians offered to invade his territories and those frontiers, they were all at peace, and traded one with another, saving only the *Iwarawaqueri* and those other nations upon the head of the river of *Caroli* called *Cassipagotos*, which we afterwards discovered, each one holding the Spaniard for a common enemy.

After he had answered thus far, he desired leave to depart, saying that he had far to go, that he was old and weak, and was every day called for by death, which was also his own phrase. I desired him to rest with us that night, but I could not entreat him; but he told me that at my return from the country above, he would again come to us, and in the meantime provide for us the best he could, of all that his country yielded. The same night he returned to *Orocotona*, his own town; so as he went that day 28 miles, the weather being very hot, the country being situate between four and five degrees of the equinoctial. This *Topiawari* is held for the proudest and wisest of all the *Orenoqueponi*, and so he behaved himself towards me in all his answers, at my return, as I marvelled to find a man of that gravity and judgment and of so good discourse, that had no help of learning nor breed.

The next morning we also left the port and sailed westward up the river, to view the famous river called *Caroli*, as well because it was marvellous of itself, as also for that I understood it led to the strongest nations of all the frontiers, that were enemies to the *Epuremei*, which are subjects to *Inca*, emperor of *Guiana* and *Manoa*. And that night we anchored at another island called *Caiama*, of some five or six miles in length; and the next day arrived at the mouth of *Caroli*. When we were short of it as low or further down as the port of *Morequito*, we heard the great roar and fall of the river. But when we came to enter with our barge and wherries, thinking to have gone up some forty miles to the nations of the *Cassipagotos*, we were not able with a barge of eight oars to row one stone's cast in an hour; and yet the river is as broad as the Thames at Woolwich, and we tried both sides and the middle and every part of the river. So as we encamped upon the banks adjoining, and sent off our *Orenoquepone* (which came with us from *Morequito*) to give knowledge to the nations upon the river of our being there, and that we desired to see the lords of *Canuria*, which dwelt within the province upon that river, making them know that we were enemies to the Spaniards (for it was on this river's side that *Morequito* slew the friar and those nine Spaniards which came from *Manoa*, the city of *Inca*, and took from them 40,000 *pesos* of gold). So as the next day there came down a lord or *cacique*, called *Wanuretona*, with many people with him, and brought all store of provisions to entertain us, as the rest had done. And as I had before made my coming known to *Topiawari*, so did I acquaint this *cacique* therewith, and how I was sent by her Majesty for the purpose aforesaid, and gathered also what I could of him touching the estate of *Guiana*. And I found that those also of *Caroli* were not only enemies to the Spaniards, but most of all to the *Epuremei*, which abound in gold. And by this *Wanuretona* I had knowledge that on the head of this river were three mighty nations, which were seated on a great lake, from whence this river descended, and were called *Cassipagotos*, *Eparagotos*, and *Arawagotos*; and that all those either against the Spaniards or the *Epuremei* would join with us, and that if we entered the land over the mountains of *Curaa* we should satisfy ourselves with gold and all other good things. He told us farther of a nation called *Iwarawaqueri*, before spoken of, that held daily war with the *Epuremei* that inhabited *Macureguarai*, the first civil town of *Guiana*, of the subjects of *Inca*, the emperor.

Upon this river one Captain *George*,[110] that I took with *Berreo*, told me that there was a great silver mine and that it was near the banks of the said river. But by this time as well *Orenoque, Caroli*, as all the rest of the rivers were risen four or five feet in height, so as it was not possible by the strength of any men, or with any boat whatsoever, to row into the river against the stream. I therefore sent Captain *Thyn*, Captain *Grenville*, my nephew *John Gilbert*, my cousin *Butshead Gorges*, Captain *Clarke*, and some thirty shot[111] more to coast the river by land and to go to a town some twenty miles over the valley called *Amnatapoi*; and if they found guides there, to go farther towards the mountain foot to another great town called *Capurepana*, belonging to a *cacique* called *Haharacoa* (that was a nephew to old *Topiawari*, king of *Aromaia*, our chiefest friend), because this town and province of *Capurepana* adjoined to *Macureguarai*, which was a frontier town of the empire. And the meanwhile, myself with Captain *Gifford*, Captain *Caulfield, Edward Hancock*, and some half a dozen shot marched overland to view the strange overfalls of the river of *Caroli*, which roared so far off; and also to see the plains adjoining and the rest of the province of *Canuri*. I sent also Captain *Whiddon, William Connock*, and some eight shot with them, to see if they could find any mineral stone alongst the river's side. When we run to[112] the tops of the first hills of the plains adjoining to the river, we beheld that wonderful breach of waters which ran down *Caroli*; and might from that mountain see the river how it ran in three parts, above twenty miles off, and there appeared some ten or twelve overfalls in sight, every one as high over the other as a church tower, which fell with that fury, that the rebound of waters made it seem as if it had been all covered over with a great shower of rain; and in some places we took it at the first for a smoke that had risen over some great town. For mine own part I was well persuaded from thence to have returned, being a very ill footman; but the rest were all so desirous to go near the said strange thunder of waters, as they drew me on by little and little, till we came into the next valley, where we might better discern the same. I never saw a more beautiful country, nor more lively prospects, hills so raised

---

[110]Alvaro Jorge, one of Berrio's officers, whose capture (and release) by Ralegh is recorded in Spanish records.
[111]Soldiers armed with muskets or other firearms.
[112]Reached, came to.

here and there over the valleys; the river winding into divers branches; the plains adjoining without bush or stubble, all fair green grass; the ground of hard sand, easy to march on, either for horse or foot; the deer crossing in every path; the birds towards the evening singing on every tree with a thousand several tunes; cranes and herons of white, crimson, and carnation, perching in the river's side; the air fresh with a gentle easterly wind; and every stone that we stooped to take up promised either gold or silver by his complexion. Your Lordship shall see of many sorts, and I hope some of them cannot be bettered under the sun; and yet we had no means but with our daggers and fingers to tear them out here and there, the rocks being most hard of that mineral spar aforesaid, and is like a flint, and is altogether as hard or harder, and besides the veins lie a fathom or two deep in the rocks. But we wanted all things requisite save only our desires and good will to have performed more if it had pleased God. To be short, when both our companies returned, each of them brought also several sorts of stones that appeared very fair, but were such as they found loose on the ground, and were for the most part but coloured, and had not any gold fixed in them. Yet such as had no judgment or experience kept all that glistered, and would not be persuaded but it was rich because of the luster; and brought of those, and of *marcasite*[113] withal, from *Trinidad*, and have delivered of those stones to be tried in many places, and have thereby bred an opinion that all the rest is of the same. Yet some of these stones I shewed afterward to a Spaniard of the *Caracas*, who told me that it was *El madre del oro*,[114] and that the mine was farther in the ground. But it shall be found a weak policy in me, either to betray myself or my country with imaginations; neither am I so far in love with that lodging, watching, care, peril, diseases, ill savours, bad fare, and many other mischiefs that accompany these voyages, as to woo myself again into any of them, were I not assured that the sun covereth not so much riches in any part of the earth. Captain *Whiddon*, and our chirurgeon,[115] *Nicholas Millechap*, brought me a kind of stones like sapphires; what they may prove I know not. I shewed them to some of the *Orenoqueponi*, and they promised to bring me to a mountain that had of them very large pieces growing diamond-wise; whether it be crystal

---

[113]A metallic sulfide that, in some forms, was commonly confused with (or passed off as) gold in Ralegh's day.

[114]The mother of gold—that is, authentic gold.

[115]Surgeon; ship physician.

of the mountain, *Bristol* diamond, or sapphire, I do not yet know, but I hope the best; sure I am that the place is as likely as those from whence all the rich stones are brought, and in the same height or very near.[116]

On the left hand of this river *Caroli* are seated those nations which are called *Iwarawakeri* before remembered, which are enemies to the *Epuremei*; and on the head of it, adjoining to the great lake *Cassipa*, are situate those other nations which also resist *Inca* and the *Epuremei*, called *Cassepagotos*, *Eparegotos*, and *Arrawagotos*. I farther understood that this lake of *Cassipa* is so large, as it is above one day's journey for one of their *canoas* to cross, which may be some forty miles; and that thereinto fall divers rivers, and that great store of grains of gold are found in the summer time when the lake falleth by the banks, in those branches.

There is also another goodly river beyond *Caroli* which is called *Arui*, which also runneth through the lake *Cassipa*, and falleth into *Orenoque* farther west, making all that land between *Caroli* and *Arui* an island; which is likewise a most beautiful country. Next unto *Arui* there are two rivers, *Atoica* and *Caora*, and on that branch which is called *Caora* are a nation of people whose heads appear not above their shoulders; which though it may be thought a mere fable, yet for mine own part I am resolved it is true, because every child in the provinces of *Arromaia* and *Canuri* affirm the same. They are called *Ewaipanoma*; they are reported to have their eyes in their shoulders and their mouths in the middle of their breasts, and that a long train of hair groweth backward between their shoulders. The son of *Topiawari*, which I brought with me into *England*, told me that they were the most mighty men of all the land, and use bows, arrows, and clubs thrice as big as any of *Guiana*, or of the *Orenoqueponi*; and that one of the *Iwarawakeri* took a prisoner of them the year before our arrival there, and brought him into the borders of *Arromaia*, his father's country. And farther, when I seemed to doubt of it, he told me that it was no wonder among them; but that they were as great a nation and as common as any other in all the provinces, and had of late years slain many hundreds of his father's people and of other nations their neighbours. But it was not my chance to hear of them till I was come

---

[116]Ralegh's reporting is accurate. The Imataca and Pakaraima ranges do contain significant sources of crystals and even diamonds. Bristol diamond is a kind of transparent rock crystal found in the Clifton limestone near Bristol, England, that is known for its diamond-like brilliancy.

away; and if I had but spoken one word of it while I was there, I might have brought one of them with me to put the matter out of doubt. Such a nation was written of by *Mandeville*, whose reports were holden for fables many years; and yet since the *East Indies* were discovered, we find his relations true of such things as heretofore were held incredible. Whether it be true or no, the matter is not great, neither can there be any profit in the imagination; for mine own part I saw them not, but I am resolved that so many people did not all combine or forethink to make the report.[117]

When I came to *Cumaná* in the *West Indies* afterwards, by chance I spake with a Spaniard dwelling not far from thence, a man of great travel. And after he knew that I had been in *Guiana*, and so far directly west as *Caroli*, the first question he asked me was whether I had seen any of the *Ewaipanoma*, which are those without heads. Who being esteemed a most honest man of his word, and in all things else, told me that he had seen many of them. I may not name him, because it may be for his disadvantage, but he is well known to *Monsieur Moucheron's* son of *London*, and to *Peter Moucheron*, merchant of the Flemish ship that was there in trade, who also heard what he avowed to be true of those people.

The fourth river to the west of *Caroli* is *Casnero*, which falleth into *Orenoque* on this side of *Amapaia*. And that river is greater than *Danubius*[118] or any of *Europe*. It riseth on the south of *Guiana* from the mountains which divide *Guiana* from *Amazones*, and I think it to be navigable many hundred miles. But we had no time, means, nor season of the year to search those rivers for the causes aforesaid, the winter being come upon us; although the winter and summer as touching cold and heat differ not, neither do the trees ever sensibly[119] lose their leaves, but have always fruit either ripe or green, and most of them both blossoms, leaves, ripe fruit, and green at one time. But their winter only consisteth of terrible rains and overflowing of the rivers, with many great storms and gusts, thunder and lightnings, of which we had our fill ere we returned.

---

[117]The keen desire to confirm indigenous reports of wondrous peoples—which were repeated to travelers for years to come and likely reflected oral traditions pertaining to enemy warriors—cost Ralegh at court, where this "fable" was mocked. It is worth noting, however, that on the Continent, this section of the text was highlighted by engravings, as the *Discovery* became associated with the very sort of wonders described by Mandeville (with whom Ralegh was sometimes published in anthologies).

[118]Danube River.

[119]Noticeably.

On the north side, the first river that falleth into the *Orenoque* is *Cari*. Beyond it, on the same side, is the river of *Limo*. Between these two is a great nation of *Cannibals*, and their chief town beareth the name of the river and is called *Acamacari*. At this town is a continual market of women for three or four hatchets apiece; they are bought by the *Arwacas*, and by them sold into the *West Indies*. To the west of *Limo* is the river *Pao*, beyond it *Caturi*, beyond that *Voari* and *Capuri*, which falleth out of the great river of *Meta*, by which *Berreo* descended from *Nuevo Reyno de Granada*.[120] To the westward of *Capuri* is the province of *Amapaia*, where *Berreo* wintered and had so many of his people poisoned with the tawny water of the marshes of the *Anebas*. Above *Amapaia*, toward *Nuevo Reyno*, fall in *Meto*, *Pato*, and *Cassanar.* To the west of those, towards the provinces of the *Ashaguas* and *Catetios*, are the rivers of *Beta*, *Dawney*, and *Ubarro*; and toward the frontier of *Peru* are the provinces of *Thomebamba* and *Caximalta*. Adjoining to *Quito* in the north of *Peru* are the rivers of *Guiacar* and *Goavar,* and on the other side of the said mountains the river of *Papamene*, which descendeth into *Marañon* or *Amazones*, passing through the province of *Mutylones*, where *Don Pedro de Osua*, who was slain by the traitor *Agiri* before rehearsed, built his brigantines when he sought *Guiana* by the way of *Amazones*.[121]

Between *Dawney* and *Beta* lieth a famous island in *Orenoque* now called *Baraquan* (for above *Meta* it is not known by the name of *Orenoque*) which is called *Athule*,[122] beyond which ships of burden cannot pass by reason of a most forcible overfall and current of waters; but in the eddy all smaller vessels may be drawn even to *Peru* itself. But to speak of more of these rivers without the description were but tedious, and therefore I will leave the rest to the description. This river of *Orenoque* is navigable for ships little less than 1,000 miles, and for lesser vessels near 2,000. By it, as aforesaid, *Peru*, *Nuevo Reyna*, and *Popayan* may be invaded; it also leadeth to the great empire of *Inca*, and to the provinces of *Amapaia* and *Anebas*, which abound in gold. His branches of *Casnero*, *Manta*, [and] *Caora* descend from the middle land and valley which lieth between the eastern province of

[120]Ralegh's geography may be imprecise, but it is identifiable. The Casnero (mentioned in the previous paragraph) is likely the Cuchivero; the Caturi, the Manapire; the Voari, the Guárico; and the Capuri, the Apure.

[121]These identifications are largely accurate (full details are provided in Harlow), even if the nomenclature has changed over the years and Ralegh has granted greater significance than necessary to some minor tributaries.

[122]The Ature cataract and rapids.

Peru and *Guiana*; and it falls into the sea between *Marañon* and *Trini-dad* in two degrees and a half. All [of] which your honours shall better perceive in the general description of *Guiana, Peru, Nuevo Reyno*, the kingdom of *Popayan*, and *Roidas*, with the province of *Venezuela*, to the bay of *Uraba*, behind *Cartagena*, westward, and to *Amazones* southward. While we lay at anchor on the coast of *Canuri*, and had taken knowledge of all the nations upon the head and branches of this river, and had found out so many several people, which were enemies to the *Epuremei* and the new conquerors, I thought it time lost to linger any longer in that place, especially for that the fury of *Orenoque* began daily to threaten us with dangers in our return. For no half day passed but the river began to rage and overflow very fearfully, and the rains came down in terrible showers, and gusts in great abundance; and withal our men began to cry out for want of shift,[123] for no man had place to bestow any other apparel than that which he wore on his back, and that was thoroughly washed on his body for the most part ten times in one day; and we had now been well near a month every day passing to the westward, farther and farther from our ships. We therefore turned towards the east and spent the rest of the time in dis-covering the river towards the sea, which we had not viewed and which was most material.

The next day following we left the mouth of *Caroli* and arrived again at the port of *Morequito* where we were before (for passing down the stream we went without labour and against the wind, little less than a hundred miles a day). As soon as I came to anchor, I sent away one for old *Topiawari*, with whom I much desired to have fur-ther conference, and also to deal with him for someone of his country to bring with us into *England*, as well to learn the language, as to con-fer withal by the way (the time being now spent of any longer stay there). Within three hours after my messenger came to him, he arrived also, and with him such a rabble of all sorts of people, and every one loaden with somewhat, as if it had been a great market or fair in *England*; and our hungry companies clustered thick and three-fold among their baskets, every one laying hand on what he liked. After he had rested a while in my tent, I shut out all but ourselves and my interpreter, and told him that I knew that both the *Epuremei* and the Spaniards were enemies to him, his country, and nations; that the one had conquered *Guiana* already, and the other sought to regain the same from them both. And therefore I desired him to instruct me

---

[123]Change of clothing.

what he could, both of the passage into the golden parts of *Guiana* and to the civil towns and apparelled people of *Inca*. He gave me an answer to this effect: first, that he did not perceive that I meant to go onward towards the city of *Manoa*, for neither the time of the year served, neither could he perceive any sufficient numbers for such an enterprise. And if I did, I was sure with all my company to be buried there, for that the emperor was of that strength, as that many times so many men more were too few. Besides, he gave me this good counsel and advised me to hold it in mind (as for himself, he knew he could not live till my return), that I should not offer by any means hereafter to invade the strong parts of *Guiana* without the help of all those nations which were also their enemies; for that it was impossible without those, either to be conducted, to be victualled, or to have aught carried with us, our people not being able to endure the march in so great heat and travail, unless the borderers gave them help to carry with them both their meat and furniture. For he remembered that in the plains of *Macureguarai* three hundred Spaniards were overthrown, who were tired out and had none of the borderers to their friends; but meeting their enemies as they passed the frontier, were environed of[124] all sides, and the people, setting the long dry grass on fire, smothered them, so as they had no breath to fight, nor could discern their enemies for the great smoke. He told me further that four days' journey from his town was *Macureguarai*, and that those were the next and nearest of the subjects of *Inca* and of the *Epuremei*, and the first town of apparelled and rich people; and that all those plates of gold which were scattered among the borderers and carried to other nations far and near came from the said *Macureguarai* and were there made, but that those of the land within were far finer, and were fashioned after the image of men, beasts, birds, and fishes. I asked him whether he thought that those companies that I had there with me were sufficient to take that town or no; he told me that he thought they were. I then asked him whether he would assist me with guides and some companies of his people to join with us; he answered that he would go himself with all the borderers if the rivers did remain fordable, upon this condition; that I would leave with him till my return again fifty soldiers, which he undertook to victual. I answered that I had not above fifty good men in all there; the rest were labourers and rowers, and that I had no provision to leave with them of powder, shot, apparel, or aught else, and that without those things necessary for

---

[124]Surrounded on.

their defence, they should be in danger of the Spaniards in my absence, who I knew would use the same measures towards mine that I offered them at *Trinidad*. And although upon the motion Captain *Caulfield*, Captain *Grenville*, my nephew *John Gilbert* and divers others were desirous to stay, yet I was resolved that they must needs have perished. For *Berreo* expected daily a supply out of *Spain*, and looked also hourly for his son to come down from *Nuevo Reyno de Granada*, with many horse and foot, and had also in *Valencia*, in the *Caracas*, two hundred horse ready to march; and I could not have spared above forty, and had not any store at all of powder, lead, or match to have left with them, nor any other provision, either spade, pickaxe, or aught else to have fortified withal.

When I had given him reason that I could not at this time leave him such a company, he then desired me to forbear[125] him and his country for that time; for he assured me that I should be no sooner three days from the coast but those *Epuremei* would invade him, and destroy all the remain of his people and friends, if he should any way either guide us or assist us against them. He further alleged that the Spaniards sought his death; and as they had already murdered his nephew *Morequito*, lord of that province, so they had him seventeen days in a chain before he was king of the country, and led him like a dog from place to place until he had paid a hundred plates of gold and divers chains of spleen-stones for his ransom. And now, since he became owner of that province, that they had many times laid wait to take him, and that they would be now more vehement when they should understand of his conference with the English. *And because,* said he, *they would the better displant me; if they cannot lay hands on me, they have gotten a nephew of mine called* Eparacano, *whom they have christened* Don Juan, *and his son* Don Pedro, *whom they have also apparelled and armed, by whom they seek to make a party against me in mine own country. He also hath taken to wife one* Louiana, *of a strong family, which are my borderers and neighbours; and myself, being now old and in the hands of death, am not able to travel nor to shift, as when I was of younger years.* He therefore prayed us to defer it till the next year, when he would undertake to draw in all the borderers to serve us, and then, also, it would be more seasonable to travel; for at this time of the year we should not be able to pass any river; the waters were and would be so grown ere our return.

He farther told me that I could not desire so much to invade

<hr/>

[125]Bear with; have patience with.

Macureguarai and the rest of *Guiana* but that the borderers would be more vehement than I. For he yielded for a chief cause that in the wars with the *Epuremei*, they were spoiled of their women, and that their wives and daughters were taken from them; so as for their own parts, they desired nothing of the gold or treasure for their labours, but only to recover women from the *Epuremei*. For he farther complained very sadly (as if it had been a matter of great consequence) that, whereas they were wont to have ten or twelve wives, they were now enforced to content themselves with three or four, and that the lords of the *Epuremei* had fifty or a hundred. And in truth they war more for women than either for gold or dominion. For the lords of countries desire many children of their own bodies to increase their races and kindreds, for in those consist their greatest trust and strength. Divers of his followers afterwards desired me to make haste again, that they might sack the *Epuremei*, and I asked them, of what? They answered, *Of their women for us, and their gold for you.* For the hope of many of those women they more desire the war than either for gold or for the recovery of their ancient territories. For what between the subjects of *Inca* and the Spaniards, those frontiers are grown thin of people; and also great numbers are fled to other nations farther off for fear of the Spaniards.

After I received this answer of the old man, we fell into consideration whether it had been of better advice to have entered *Macureguarai*, and to have begun a war upon *Inca* at this time, yea or no, if the time of the year and all things else had sorted. For mine own part (as we were not able to march it for the rivers, neither had any such strength as was requisite, and durst not abide the coming of the winter or to tarry any longer from our ships) I thought it very evil counsel to have attempted it at that time, although the desire of gold will answer many objections. But it would have been, in mine opinion, an utter overthrow to the enterprise, if the same should be hereafter by her Majesty attempted. For then (whereas now they have heard we were enemies to the Spaniards and were sent by her Majesty to relieve them) they would as good cheap[126] have joined with the Spaniards at our return, as to have yielded unto us, when they had proved that we came both for one errand, and that both sought but to sack and spoil them. But as yet our desire of gold, or our purpose of invasion, is not known unto those of the empire. And it is likely that if her Majesty undertake the enterprise, they will rather submit themselves

---

[126]With little trouble or effort.

to her obedience than to the Spaniards, of whose cruelty both themselves and the borderers have already tasted. And therefore, till I had known her Majesty's pleasure, I would rather have lost the sack of one or two towns, although they might have been very profitable, than to have defaced or endangered the future hope of so many millions, and the great good and rich trade which *England* may be possessed of thereby. I am assured now that they will all die, even to the last man, against the Spaniards in hope of our succour and return. Whereas, otherwise, if I had either laid hands on the borderers or ransomed the lords, as *Berreo* did, or invaded the subjects of *Inca*, I know all had been lost for hereafter.

After that I had resolved *Topiawari*, lord of *Aromaia*, that I could not at this time leave with him the companies he desired, and that I was contented to forbear the enterprise against the *Epuremei* till the next year, he freely gave me his only son to take with me into *England* and hoped that though he himself had but a short time to live, yet that by our means his son should be established after his death.[127] And I left with him one *Francis Sparrow*, a servant of Captain *Gifford* (who was desirous to tarry and could describe a country with his pen), and a boy of mine called *Hugh Goodwin*, to learn the language. I after asked the manner how the *Epuremei* wrought those plates of gold, and how they could melt it out of the stone. He told me that the most of the gold which they made in plates and images was not severed from the stone, but that on the lake of *Manoa*, and in a multitude of other rivers, they gathered it in grains of perfect gold and in pieces as big as small stones; and that they put to it a part of copper, otherwise they could not work it; and that they used a great earthen pot with holes round about it, and when they had mingled the gold and copper together, they fastened canes to the holes, and so with the breath of men they increased the fire till the metal ran, and then they cast it into moulds of stone and clay, and so make those plates and images. I have sent your honours of two sorts such as I could by chance recover, more to shew the manner of them than for the value. For I did not in any sort make my desire of gold known, because I had neither time nor power to have a greater quantity. I gave among them many more pieces of gold than I received, of the new money of twenty shillings with her Majesty's picture, to wear, with promise that they would become her servants thenceforth.

I have also sent your honours of the ore, whereof I know some is as

---

[127]This son was Iwiakanarie Gualtero, "Gualtero" being a Spanish term for Walter Ralegh.

rich as the earth yieldeth any, of which I know there is sufficient, if nothing else were to be hoped for. But besides that we were not able to tarry and search the hills, for we had neither pioneers,[128] bars, sledges, nor wedges of iron to break the ground, without which there is no working in mines. But we saw all the hills with stones of the colour of gold and silver, and we tried them to be no *marcasite*, and therefore such as the Spaniards call *El madre del oro*, which is an undoubted assurance of the general abundance; and myself saw the outside of many mines of the white spar, which I know to be the same that all covet in this world, and of those more than I will speak of.

Having learned what I could in *Canuri* and *Aromaia*, and received a faithful promise of the principallest of those provinces to become servants to her Majesty, and to resist the Spaniards if they made any attempt in our absence, and that they would draw in the nations about the lake of *Cassipa* and those of *Iwarawaqueri*, I then parted from old *Topiawari* and received his son for a pledge between us, and left with him two of ours as aforesaid. To *Francis Sparrow* I gave instructions to travel to *Macureguarai* with such merchandises as I left with him, thereby to learn the place and, if it were possible, to go on to the great city of *Manoa*. Which being done, we weighed anchor and coasted the river on *Guiana* side, because we came upon the north side, by the lawns of the *Saima* and *Wikiri*.

There came with us from *Aromaia* a *cacique* called *Putijma*, that commanded the province of *Warapana* (which *Putijma* slew the nine Spaniards upon *Caroli* before spoken of) who desired us to rest at the port of his country, promising to bring us to a mountain adjoining to his town that had stones of the colour of gold, which he performed. And after we had rested there one night, I went myself in the morning with most of the gentlemen of my company overland towards the said mountain, marching by a river's side called *Mana*, leaving on the right hand a town called *Tuteritona*, standing in the province of *Tarracoa*, of which *Wariaaremagoto* is principal. Beyond it lieth another town towards the south, in the valley of *Amariocapana*, which beareth the name of the said valley, whose plains stretch themselves some sixty miles in length, east and west, as fair ground and as beautiful fields as any man hath ever seen, with divers copses scattered here and there by the river's side, and all as full of deer as any forest or park in *England*, and in every lake and river the like abundance of fish and fowl; of which *Irraparragota* is lord.[129]

---

[128]Diggers or miners.
[129]Ralegh is describing the plains of Upata and Piacoa.

From the river of *Mana*, we crossed another river in the said beautiful valley called *Oiana*, and rested ourselves by a clear lake which lay in the middle of the said *Oiana*; and one of our guides kindling us fire with two sticks, we stayed a while to dry our shirts, which with the heat hung very wet and heavy on our shoulders. Afterwards we sought the ford to pass over towards the mountain called *Iconuri*, where *Putijma* foretold us of the mine. In this lake we saw one of the great fishes, as big as a wine pipe,[130] which they call *manati*, and is most excellent and wholesome meat. But after I perceived that to pass the said river would require half a day's march more, I was not able myself to endure it, and therefore I sent Captain *Keymis* with six shot to go on, and gave him order not to return to the port of *Putijma*, which is called *Chiparepare*, but to take leisure, and to march down the said valley as far as a river called *Cumaca*, where I promised to meet him again (*Putijma* himself promising also to be his guide). And as they marched, they left the towns of *Emparepana* and *Capurepana* on the right hand, and marched from *Putijma's* house, down the said valley of *Amariocapana*; and we, returning the same day to the river's side, saw by the way many rocks like unto gold ore, and on the left hand a round mountain which consisted of mineral stone.

From hence we rowed down the stream, coasting the province of *Parino*. As for the branches of rivers which I overpass in this discourse, those shall be better expressed in the description, with the mountains of *Aio*, *Ara*, and the rest, which are situate in the provinces of *Parino* and *Carricurrina*. When we were come as far down as the land called *Ariacoa*, where *Orenoque* divideth itself into three great branches, each of them being most goodly rivers, I sent away Captain *Henry Thyn* and Captain *Grenville* with the galley, the nearest way, and took with me Captain *Gifford*, Captain *Caulfield*, *Edward Porter*, and Captain *Eynos* with mine own barge and the two wherries, and went down that branch of *Orenoque* which is called *Cararoopana*, which leadeth towards *Emeria*, the province of *Carapana*, and towards the east sea, as well to find out Captain *Keymis*, whom I had sent overland, as also to acquaint myself with *Carapana*, who is one of the greatest of all the lords of the *Orenoqueponi*. And when we came to the river of *Cumaca*, to which *Putijma* promised to conduct Captain *Keymis*, I left Captain *Eynos* and Master *Porter* in the said river to expect his coming, and the rest of us rowed down the stream towards *Emeria*.

---

[130] A large cask equal to four barrels, or about 477.5 liters.

In this branch called *Cararoopana* were also many goodly islands, some of six miles long, some of ten, and some of twenty. When it grew towards sunset, we entered a branch of a river that fell into *Orenoque*, called *Winicapora*, where I was informed of the mountain of crystal, to which in truth for the length of the way, and the evil season of the year, I was not able to march, nor abide any longer upon the journey. We saw it afar off, and it appeared like a white church tower of an exceeding height. There falleth over it a mighty river which toucheth no part of the side of the mountain, but rusheth over the top of it, and falleth to the ground with a terrible noise and clamour, as if a thousand great bells were knocked one against another. I think there is not in the world so strange an overfall, nor so wonderful to behold. *Berreo* told me that it hath diamonds and other precious stones on it, and that they shined very far off; but what it hath I know not, neither durst he or any of his men ascend to the top of the said mountain, those people adjoining being his enemies (as they were) and the way to it so impassable.

Upon this river of *Winicapora* we rested a while, and from thence marched into the country to a town called after the name of the river, whereof the chief was one *Timitwara*, who also offered to conduct me to the top of the said mountain called *Wacarima*. But when we came in first to the house of the said *Timitwara*, being upon one of their feast days, we found them all as drunk as beggars, and the pots[131] walking from one to another without rest. We that were weary and hot with marching were glad of the plenty, though a small quantity satisfied us, their drink being very strong and heady, and so rested ourselves a while. After we had fed, we drew ourselves back to our boats upon the river, and there came to us all the lords of the country, with all such kind of victual as the place yielded, and with their delicate wine of *pinas*, and with abundance of hens and other provisions, and of those stones which we call spleen-stones. We understood by these chieftains of *Winicapora* that their Lord *Carapana* was departed from *Emeria*, which was now in sight, and that he was fled to *Cairamo*, adjoining to the mountains of *Guiana*, over the valley called *Amariocapana*, being persuaded by those ten Spaniards which lay at his house that we would destroy him and his country. But after these *caciques* of *Winicapora* and *Saporatona* his followers perceived our purpose, and saw that we came as enemies to the Spaniards only, and had not so much as harmed any of those nations, no, though we found them to be of

---

[131] Drinking vessels.

the Spaniards' own servants, they assured us that *Carapana* would be as ready to serve us as any of the lords of the provinces which we had passed; and that he durst do no other till this day but entertain the Spaniards, his country lying so directly in their way, and next of all other to any entrance that should be made in *Guiana* on that side. And they further assured us that it was not for fear of our coming that he was removed, but to be acquitted of those Spaniards or any other that should come hereafter. For the province of *Cairoma* is situate at the mountain foot, which divideth the plains of *Guiana* from the countries of the *Orenoqueponi*; by means whereof if any should come in our absence into his towns, he would slip over the mountains into the plains of *Guiana* among the *Epuremei*, where the Spaniards durst not follow him without great force. But in mine opinion, or rather I assure myself, that *Carapana* (being a notable wise and subtle fellow, a man of one hundred years of age and therefore of great experience) is removed to look on, and if he find that we return strong he will be ours; if not, he will excuse his departure to the Spaniards, and say it was for fear of our coming.

We therefore thought it bootless[132] to row so far down the stream, or to seek any farther for this old fox; and therefore from the river of *Waricapana*, which lieth at the entrance of *Emeria*, we turned again, and left to the eastward those four rivers which fall from out the mountains of *Emeria* into *Orenoque*, which are *Waracapari*, *Coirama*, *Akaniri*, and *Iparoma*. Below those four are also these branches and mouths of *Orenoque*, which fall into the east sea, whereof the first is *Araturi*, the next *Amacura*, the third *Barima*, the fourth *Wana*, the fifth *Morooca*, the sixth *Paroma*, the last *Wijmi*. Beyond them there fall out of the land between *Orenoque* and *Amazones* fourteen rivers, which I forbear to name, inhabited by the *Arwacas* and *Cannibals*.[133]

It is now time to return towards the north, and we found it a wearisome way back from the borders of *Emeria*, to recover up again to the head of the river *Carerupana*, by which we descended, and where we parted from the galley, which I directed to take the next way to the port of *Toparimaca*, by which we entered first.

All the night it was stormy and dark, and full of thunder and great

---

[132]Unprofitable or useless.

[133]Scholars have attempted to identify this dizzying array of place names, but this may miss Ralegh's chief point: to offer a flood of geographic and strategic data that would not only serve colonial planners in England but also demonstrate his thorough "discoveries."

showers, so as we were driven to keep close by the banks in our small boats, being all heartily afraid both of the billow and terrible current of the river. By the next morning we recovered the mouth of the river of *Cumaca*, where we left Captain *Eynos* and *Edward Porter* to attend the coming of Captain *Keymis* overland; but when we entered the same, they had heard no news of his arrival, which bred in us a great doubt what might be become of him. I rowed up a league or two farther into the river, shooting off pieces all the way, that he might know of our being there; and the next morning we heard them answer us also with a piece. We took them aboard us and took our leave of *Putijma*, their guide, who of all others most lamented our departure, and offered to send his son with us into *England*, if we could have stayed till he had sent back to his town. But our hearts were cold to behold the great rage and increase of *Orenoque*, and therefore [we] departed and turned toward the west, till we had recovered the parting of the three branches aforesaid, that we might put down the stream after the galley.

The next day we landed on the island of *Assapana*, which divideth the river from that branch by which we sent down to *Emeria*, and there feasted ourselves with that beast which is called *armadillo*, presented unto us before at *Winicapora*. And the day following, we recovered the galley at anchor at the port of *Toparimaca*, and the same evening departed with very foul weather, and terrible thunder and showers, for the winter was come on very far. The best was, we went no less than 100 miles a day down the river; but by the way we entered, it was impossible to return, for that the river of *Amana*, being in the bottom of the bay of *Guanipa*, cannot be sailed back by any means, both the breeze and current of the sea were so forcible. And therefore we followed a branch of *Orenoque* called *Capuri*, which entered into the sea eastward of our ships, to the end we might bear with them before the wind; and it was not without need, for we had by that way as much to cross of the main sea, after we came to the river's mouth, as between *Gravelin* and *Dover*, in such boats as your Honours have heard.

To speak of what passed homeward were tedious, either to describe or name any of the rivers, islands, or villages of the *Tivitivas*, which dwell on trees; we will leave all those to the general map. And to be short, when we were arrived at the sea-side, then grew our greatest doubt, and the bitterest of all our journey forepassed; for I protest before God, that we were in a most desperate estate. For the same night which we anchored in the mouth of the river of *Capuri*, where it falleth into the sea, there arose a mighty storm, and the river's mouth was at least a league broad; so as we ran before night close under the land with our small boats and brought the galley as near as we could. But she had as much ado to live as could be, and there wanted little of her sinking, and all those in her; for mine own part, I confess, I was very doubtful which way to take, either to go over in the pestered galley, there being but six foot water over the sands for two leagues together, and that also in the channel, and she drew five; or to adventure in so great a billow, and in so doubtful weather, to cross the seas in my barge. The longer we tarried, the worse it was; and therefore I took Captain *Gifford*, Captain *Caulfield*, and my cousin *Grenville* into my barge; and after it cleared up about midnight we put ourselves to God's keeping, and thrust out into the sea, leaving the galley at anchor, who durst not adventure but by daylight. And so, being all very sober and melancholy, one faintly cheering another to shew courage, it pleased God that the next day about nine of the clock, we descried the island of *Trinidad*; and steering for the nearest part of it, we kept the shore till we came to *Curiapan*, where we found our ships at anchor, then which there was never to us a more joyful sight.

Now that it hath pleased God to send us safe to our ships, it is time to leave *Guiana* to the sun, whom they worship, and steer away towards the north. I will, therefore, in a few words finish the discovery thereof. Of the several nations which we found upon this discovery, I will once again make repetition and how they are affected. At our first entrance into *Amana*, which is one of the outlets of *Orenoque*, we left on the right hand of us in the bottom of the bay, lying directly against *Trinidad*, a nation of inhuman *Cannibals*, which inhabit the rivers of *Guanipa* and *Berbeese*. In the same bay there is also a third river, which is called *Areo*, which riseth on *Paria* side towards *Cumaná*, and that river is inhabited with the *Wikiri*, whose chief town upon the said river is *Sayma*. In this bay there are no more rivers but these three before rehearsed and the four branches of *Amana*, all which in the winter thrust so great abundance of water into the sea, as the same is taken up fresh two or three leagues from the land. In the passages towards *Guiana* (that is, in all those lands which the eight branches of *Orenoque* fashion into islands) there are but one sort of people, called *Tivitivas*, but of two castes, as they term them, the one called *Ciawani*, the other *Waraweeti*, and those war one with the other.

On the hithermost part of *Orenoque*, as at *Toparimaca* and *Winicapora*, those are of a nation called *Nepoios*, and are the followers of *Carapana*, lord of *Emeria*. Between *Winicapora* and the port of *Morequito*, which standeth in *Aromaia*, and all those in the valley of *Amarioca-pana* are called *Orenoqueponi*, and did obey *Morequito*, and are now followers of *Topiawari*. Upon the river of *Caroli* are the *Canuri*, which are governed by a woman (who is inheritrix of that province), who came far off to see our nation and asked me divers questions of her Majesty, being much delighted with the discourse of her Majesty's greatness, and wondering at such reports as we truly made of her Highness' many virtues. And upon the head of *Caroli* and on the lake of *Cassipa* are the three strong nations of the *Cassipagotos*. Right south into the land are the *Capurepani* and *Emparepani*, and beyond those, adjoining to *Macureguarai*, the first city of *Inca*, are the *Iwarawakeri*. All these are professed enemies to the Spaniards, and to the rich *Epuremei* also. To the west of *Caroli* are divers nations of *Cannibals* and of those *Ewaipanoma* without heads. Directly west are the *Ama-paias* and *Anebas*, which are also marvellous rich in gold. The rest towards *Peru* we will omit. On the north of *Orenoque*, between it and the *West Indies*, are the *Wikiri, Saymi*, and the rest before spoken of, all mortal enemies to the Spaniards. On the south side of the main mouth of *Orenoque* are the *Arwacas*; and beyond them, the *Cannibals*; and to the south of them, the *Amazones*.

To make mention of the several beasts, birds, fishes, fruits, flowers, gums, sweet woods, and of their several religions and customs would for the first require as many volumes as those of *Gesnerus*, and for the next another bundle of *Decades*.[134] The religion of the *Epuremei* is the same which the *Incas*, emperors of *Peru*, used, which may be read in *Cieza*[135] and other Spanish stories: how they believe the immortality of the soul, worship the sun, and bury with them alive their best beloved wives and treasure, as they likewise do in *Pegu* in the *East Indies* and other places. The *Orenoqueponi* bury not their wives with them, but their jewels, hoping to enjoy them again. The *Arwacas* dry the bones of their lords, and their wives and friends drink them in powder. In the graves of the *Peruvians*, the Spaniards found their greatest abundance of treasure. The like also is to be found among these people in every province. They have all many wives, and the lords five-fold to the common sort. Their wives never eat with their husbands, nor among the men, but serve their husbands at meals and afterwards feed by them-

---

[134]The references are to Conrad Gesner's five-volume *Historiae Animalium* (1551–1587) and Pietro Martire d'Anghiera's eight-part history of the conquest, *De orbe novo* (1530).

[135]Cieza de Léon (see note 27).

selves. Those that are past their younger years make all their bread and drink, and work their cotton-beds, and do all else of service and labour; for the men do nothing but hunt, fish, play, and drink, when they are out of the wars.

I will enter no further into discourse of their manners, laws, and customs. And because I have not myself seen the cities of *Inca*, I cannot avow on my credit what I have heard, although it be very likely that the emperor *Inca* hath built and erected as magnificent palaces in *Guiana* as his ancestors did in *Peru*; which were for their riches and rareness most marvellous, and exceeding all in *Europe*, and, I think, of the world, *China* excepted, which also the Spaniards (which I had) assured me to be of truth, as also the nations of the borderers, who, being but *Salvaios*[136] to those of the inland, do cause much treasure to be buried with them. For I was informed of one of the *caciques* of the valley of *Amariocapana* which had buried with him a little before our arrival a chair of gold most curiously wrought, which was made either in *Macureguarai* adjoining or in *Manoa*. But if we should have grieved them in their religion at the first, before they had been taught better, and have digged up their graves, we had lost them all. And therefore I held my first resolution, that her Majesty should either accept or refuse the enterprise ere anything should be done that might in any sort hinder the same. And if *Peru* had so many heaps of gold, whereof those *Incas* were princes and that they delighted so much therein, no doubt but this which now liveth and reigneth in *Manoa* hath the same humour and, I am assured, hath more abundance of gold within his territory than all *Peru* and the *West Indies*.

For the rest, which myself have seen, I will promise these things that follow and I know to be true. Those that are desirous to discover and to see many nations may be satisfied within this river, which bringeth forth so many arms and branches leading to several countries and provinces, above 2,000 miles east and west and 800 miles south and north; and of these the most either rich in gold or in other merchandises. The common soldier shall here fight for gold and pay himself, instead of pence, with plates of half a foot broad, whereas he breaketh his bones in other wars for provant and penury.[137] Those

---

[136] *Salvaios* has been read to mean "savages" (cf. *salvajes*), yet it may also be the name of an ethnolinguistic group. Ralegh meant to indicate, in all cases, a cultural distinction between coastal and inland Indians, the latter seen as more "civil" (that is, inclined to build magnificent palaces) than the former.

[137] Basic provisions (allowance of food) and poverty.

commanders and chieftains that shoot at honour and abundance shall find there more rich and beautiful cities, more temples adorned with golden images, more sepulchres filled with treasure, than either *Cortez* found in *Mexico* or *Pizarro* in *Peru*. And the shining glory of this conquest will eclipse all those so far extended beams of the Spanish nation. There is no country which yieldeth more pleasure to the inhabitants, either for those common delights of hunting, hawking, fishing, fowling, and the rest than *Guiana* doth. It hath so many plains, clear rivers, abundance of pheasants, partridges, quails, rails, cranes, herons, and all other fowl; deer of all sorts, porks, hares, lions, tigers, leopards, and divers other sorts of beasts, either for chase or food. It hath a kind of beast called *cama* or *anta*,[138] as big as an English beef, and in great plenty.

To speak of the several sorts of every kind I fear would be troublesome to the reader, and therefore I will omit them and conclude that, both for health, good air, pleasure, and riches, I am resolved it cannot be equalled by any region either in the east or west. Moreover the country is so healthful, as [of] a hundred persons and more (which lay without shift most sluttishly,[139] and were every day almost melted with heat in rowing and marching, and suddenly wet again with great showers, and did eat of all sorts of corrupt fruits, and made meals of fresh fish without seasoning, of *tortugas*, of *lagartos*, and of all sorts good and bad, without either order or measure, and besides lodged in the open air every night), we lost not any one, nor had one ill-disposed to my knowledge; nor found any *calentura*[140] or other of those pestilent diseases which dwell in all hot regions, and so near the equinoctial line.

Where there is store of gold, it is in effect needless to remember other commodities for trade. But it hath, towards the south part of the river, great quantities of brazil wood and divers berries that dye a most perfect crimson and carnation; and for painting, all *France, Italy*, or the *East Indies* yield none such. For the more the skin is washed, the fairer the colour appeareth, and with which even those brown and tawny women spot themselves and colour their cheeks.[141] All places yield abundance of cotton, of silk, of *balsam*, and of those kinds most excellent and never known in *Europe*; of all sorts of gums, of Indian

---

[138]Tapir.

[139]Slovenly or unkempt; without good hygiene.

[140]A disease common to sailors in the tropics, characterized by delirium; fever or severe sunstroke.

[141]Ralegh had in mind annatto, an orange-red dye used for cloth and foods (such as cheese) and traded by the Dutch from the seventeenth century.

pepper; and what else the countries may afford within the land we know not, neither had we time to abide the trial and search. The soil besides is so excellent and so full of rivers, as it will carry sugar, ginger, and all those other commodities which the *West Indies* hath.

The navigation is short, for it may be sailed with an ordinary wind in six weeks, and in the like time back again. And by the way neither lee-shore,[142] enemies' coast, rocks, nor sands, all which in the voyages to the *West Indies* and all other places we are subject unto; as the channel of *Bahama*, coming from the *West Indies*, cannot be passed in the winter, and when it is at the best, it is a perilous and a fearful place; the rest of the *Indies* for calms and diseases very troublesome, and the *Bermudas* a hellish sea for thunder, lightning, and storms.

This very year there were seventeen sail of Spanish ships lost in the channel of *Bahama*, and the great *Philip*, like to have sunk at the *Bermudas*, was put back to *St. Juan de Puerto Rico*. And so it falleth out in that navigation every year for the most part, which in this voyage are not to be feared; for the time of year to leave *England* is best in July, and the summer in *Guiana* is in October, November, December, January, February, and March; and then the ships may depart thence in April, and so return again into *England* in June. So as they shall never be subject to winter weather, either coming, going, or staying there; which, for my part, I take to be one of the greatest comforts and encouragements that can be thought on, having, as I have done, tasted in this voyage by the *West Indies* so many calms, so much heat, such outrageous gusts, foul weather, and contrary winds.

To conclude, *Guiana* is a country that hath yet her maidenhead, never sacked, turned, nor wrought; the face of the earth hath not been torn, nor the virtue and salt of the soil spent by manurance. The graves have not been opened for gold, the mines not broken with sledges, nor their images pulled down out of their temples. It hath never been entered by any army of strength, and never conquered or possessed by any Christian prince. It is besides so defensible, that if two forts be builded in one of the provinces which I have seen, the flood setteth in so near the bank, where the channel also lieth, that no ship can pass up but within a pike's length of the artillery, first of the one, and afterwards of the other. Which two forts will be a sufficient guard both to the empire of *Inca*, and to a hundred other several kingdoms lying within the said river, even to the city of *Quito* in *Peru*.

---

[142] A shore toward which the wind blows, making for difficult sailing.

There is therefore great difference between the easiness of the conquest of *Guiana* and the defence of it being conquered, and the *West* or *East Indies*. *Guiana* hath but one entrance by the sea (if it have that) for any vessels of burden. So as whosoever shall first possess it, it shall be found unaccessible for any enemy, except he come in wherries, barges, or *canoas*, or else in flat-bottomed boats. And if he do offer to enter it in that manner, the woods are so thick 200 miles together upon the rivers of such entrance, as a mouse cannot sit in a boat unhit from the bank. By land it is more impossible to approach; for it hath the strongest situation of any region under the sun and is so environed with impassable mountains on every side, as it is impossible to victual any company in the passage. Which hath been well proved by the Spanish nation, who since the conquest of *Peru* have never left five years free from attempting this empire, or discovering some way into it; and yet of 23 several gentlemen, knights, and noblemen, there was never any that knew which way to lead an army by land, or to conduct ships by sea, anything near the said country. *Oreliano*, of which the river of *Amazones* taketh name, was the first, and *Don Antonio de Berreo*, whom we displanted, the last: and I doubt much whether he himself or any of his yet know the best way into the said empire. It can therefore hardly be regained, if any strength be formerly set down, but in one or two places, and but two or three crumsters[143] or galleys built and furnished upon the river within. The *West Indies* hath many ports, watering places, and landings; and nearer than 300 miles to *Guiana*, no man can harbour a ship, except he know one only place, which is not learned in haste, and which, I will undertake, there is not any one of my companies that knoweth, whosoever hearkened most after it.

Besides, by keeping one good fort, or building one town of strength, the whole empire is guarded; and whatsoever companies shall be afterwards planted within the land, although in twenty several provinces, those shall be able all to reunite themselves upon any occasion either by the way of one river, or be able to march by land without either wood, bog, or mountain. Whereas in the *West Indies* there are few towns or provinces that can succour or relieve one the other, either by land or sea. By land the countries are either desert, mountainous, or strong enemies. By sea, if any man invade to the eastward, those to the west cannot in many months turn against the breeze and eastern wind. Besides, the Spaniards are therein so dispersed as they

---

[143]A kind of galley or hoy (that is, a small vessel usually rigged as a sloop).

are nowhere strong, but in *Nueva Hispania* only; the sharp mountains, the thorns and poisoned prickles, the sandy and deep ways in the valleys, the smothering heat and air, and want of water in other places are their only and best defence; which (because those nations that invade them are not victualled or provided to stay, neither have any place to friend adjoining) do serve them instead of good arms and great multitudes.

The *West Indies* were first offered her Majesty's grandfather by *Columbus*, a stranger in whom there might be doubt of deceit;[144] and besides it was then thought incredible that there were such and so many lands and regions never written of before. This Empire is made known to her Majesty by her own vassal, and by him that oweth to her more duty than an ordinary subject; so that it shall ill sort with the many graces and benefits which I have received to abuse her Highness, either with fables or imaginations. The country is already discovered, many nations won to her Majesty's love and obedience, and those Spaniards which have latest and longest laboured about the conquest, beaten out, discouraged, and disgraced, which among these nations were thought invincible. Her Majesty may in this enterprise employ all those soldiers and gentlemen that are younger brethren, and all captains and chieftains that want employment, and the charge will be only the first setting out in victualling and arming them; for after the first or second year I doubt not but to see in *London* a Contractation house[145] of more receipt for *Guiana* than there is now in *Seville* for the *West Indies*.

And I am resolved that if there were but a small army afoot in *Guiana*, marching towards *Manoa*, the chief city of *Inca*, he would yield [to] her Majesty by composition[146] so many hundred thousand pounds yearly as should both defend all enemies abroad and defray all expenses at home; and that he would besides pay a garrison of three or four thousand soldiers very royally to defend him against other nations. For he cannot but know how his predecessors, yea, how his own great uncles, *Guascar* and *Atabalipa*, sons to *Cuanacapa*, emperor of *Peru*, were (while they contended for the empire) beaten out by the Spaniards, and that both of late years and ever since the said conquest,

---

[144]The reference is to Columbus's offer of service to Henry VII, grandfather of Queen Elizabeth, prior to his voyage for Queen Isabel of Spain. Note that Ralegh ultimately played the role of Columbus by also offering his services to Elizabeth.

[145]The famous *Casa de Contratación*, or customshouse, in Seville, which functioned as the administrative nerve center of Spain's overseas empire.

[146]Mutual arrangement or agreement.

the Spaniards have sought the passages and entry of his country; and of their cruelties used to the borderers he cannot be ignorant. In which respects no doubt but he will be brought to tribute with great gladness; if not, he hath neither shot nor iron weapon in all his empire, and therefore may easily be conquered.

And I further remember that *Berreo* confessed to me and others, which I protest before the Majesty of God to be true, that there was found among prophecies in *Peru* (at such time as the empire was reduced to the Spanish obedience), in their chiefest temples, amongst divers others which foreshowed the loss of the said empire, that from *Inglatierra*[147] those *Incas* should be again in time to come restored and delivered from the servitude of the said conquerors. And I hope, as we with these few hands have displanted the first garrison and driven them out of the said country, so her Majesty will give order for the rest, and either defend it, and hold it as tributary, or conquer and keep it as empress of the same. For whatsoever prince shall possess it, shall be greatest; and if the king of *Spain* enjoy it, he will become unresistible. Her Majesty hereby shall confirm and strengthen the opinions of all nations as touching her great and princely actions. And where the south border of *Guiana* reacheth to the dominion and empire of the *Amazones*, those women shall hereby hear the name of a virgin, which is not only able to defend her own territories and her neighbours, but also to invade and conquer so great empires and so far removed.

To speak more at this time I fear would be but troublesome: I trust in God, this being true, will suffice, and that he which is King of all Kings, and Lord of Lords, will put it into her heart which is Lady of Ladies to possess it. If not, I will judge those men worthy to be kings thereof, that by her grace and leave will undertake it of themselves.

[147]England.

PART THREE

Related Documents

1

Picturing Ralegh: Courtly Self-Fashioning
1588–1735

Ralegh and his contemporaries loved pictures. They were visually "liter-ate" and imagined that other cultures shared their faith in the efficacy of mimetic representation. This may be why Ralegh, in the middle of the Orinoco River, decided to show the Guianans "her Majesty's picture," a visual prompt that would convert them, he imagined, to the English cause (page 50). Like any modern politician, Ralegh carefully managed his own public image and enlisted visual media to do so. He used paint-ings, especially, to "fashion" his persona: to advertise his military and exploratory successes, his elevated standing at court, and, not least, his famous good looks. Paintings were a relatively elite source—unlike prints, they did not circulate widely—yet they had a vital impact on Ralegh's target audience at court. Ralegh's main viewer, arguably, was the queen herself, and his earliest portraits (which Ralegh would have commissioned himself) display a vigorously handsome courtier in his prime. The oval miniature of circa 1585 (see Figure 1, page 5) was done by the royal portraitist Nicholas Hilliard, in the fashionable style of the day. It conveys both the elegance of the dashing favorite—note the extravagant lace and sharp goatee—and the physical impressiveness of

Ralegh, whose broad shoulders fill the picture frame. Another portrait (see cover image) shows Ralegh as an explorer. The globe, compass, and naval sketch (in the rear) emphasize his expert knowledge, while the sword and (as always) dashing cloak express martial prowess. Many of these themes would carry over in later paintings and printed engravings, the latter circulating throughout Europe. Indeed, many of Ralegh's early efforts to control his image paid dividends later in life: he was almost uniformly shown in heroic poses, associated with noble deeds, and cloaked in stylish costumes. These images underscored his courtly and military status and, above all, the favor he had won from the queen.

Figure 2. Sir Walter Ralegh, *1588, attributed to "H" monogrammist.*

This magnificent portrait done in the Armada year glorifies Ralegh at the
height of his power. Note not only the lavish costume—pearls, brocaded vest,
fur trim—but also the moon in the upper left corner. This was the emblem
of Cynthia, aka Queen Elizabeth, who bestowed on her servant Sir Walter
Ralegh whatever magnificence he had.

National Portrait Gallery, London, oil on panel (914 mm × 746 mm).

Figure 3.   Sir Walter Ralegh, *ca. 1590, attributed to workshop of Marcus Gheeraerts.*

Ralegh had himself painted as captain of the guard, a position that afforded both prestige and access to the queen. He wears so-called Greenwich armor, fashionable among young courtiers of the time, with richly brocaded and pearled trunks. Signs of power abound: the plumed helmet, military baton, and (in the rear) tent with coat of arms.

Colonial Williamsburg Foundation (acc. no. 1938-147), oil on panel (44³/₁₆" × 33⅞").

116

Figure 4. Sir Walter Raleigh Knt., *1735, George Vertue, engraving.*

This engraving, produced more than a century after Ralegh's death, shows how his image had by then been codified (note especially the resemblance to Figure 3). The armor, baton, and globe all allude to Ralegh's martial reputation, while the books speak to his learning. The globe shows the region of Guiana, while the maps illustrate sites of Ralegh's anti-Spanish heroics in Cádiz and the Azores. By these later years, when England was vehemently anti-Catholic, Ralegh's bona fides as a Protestant warrior may have trumped his status as an American explorer.

National Portrait Gallery, London.

2

SIR WALTER RALEGH

Farewell to the Court and *The Lie*

ca. 1588 and ca. 1592

Ralegh was phenomenally versatile, and among his considerable talents was writing poetry. To be a poet in Elizabethan England was not so much a career choice as a mark of breeding, education, social standing, and, naturally, verbal wit. Ralegh composed his fair share of love lyrics and occasional verse—poems to mark the publication of Spenser's Faerie Queene, *for example—and he is well known for his admiring poem to the queen,* The Ocean to Cynthia, *which survives in fragments. Much of what he wrote, however, was a good deal sharper and world-weary, poems that convey the frustration of the lover or the thwarted ambitions of the courtier. "Farewell to the Court," likely written before Ralegh's famous fall from grace, expresses a prescient sense of regret. "The Lie" rails against all manner of pretension, suggesting the poet's disillusion and even contempt. It ranks among Ralegh's most powerful poems and provoked several responses.*[1]

Farewell to the Court (ca. 1588)

Like truthless dreams, so are my joys expired,
And past return are all my dandled[2] days;
My love misled, and fancy quite retired,
Of all which passed the sorrow only stays.

---

[1] As with nearly all Elizabethan poetry, questions of attribution complicate ascribing works even to as prominent a figure as Ralegh. For guidance, I have followed the most recent (and excellent) edition of Michael Rudick, ed., *The Poems of Sir Walter Ralegh: A Historical Edition*, Renaissance English Text Society, 7th ser., 23 (Tempe: Arizona Center for Medieval and Renaissance Studies, 1999), which accepts both of these poems and offers scholarly details pertaining to their authorship and composition.
[2] Pampered; youthful.

My lost delights, now clean from sight of land,
Have left me all alone in unknown ways:
My mind to woe, my life in fortune's hand,
Of all which passed the sorrow only stays.

As in a country strange, without companion,
I only wail the wrong of death's delays,
Whose sweet spring spent, whose summer well nigh done,
Of all which passed only the sorrow stays.

Whom care forewarns, ere age and winter cold,
To haste me hence to find my fortune's fold.

The Lie (ca. 1592)

Go, Soul, the body's guest,
Upon a thankless errand;
Fear not to touch the best;
The truth shall be thy warrant:
Go, since I needs must die,
And give the world the lie.

Say to the court, it glows
And shines like rotten wood;
Say to the church, it shows
What's good, and doth no good:
If church and court reply,
Then give them both the lie.

Tell potentates, they live
Acting by others' action;
Not loved unless they give,
Not strong but by a faction.
If potentates reply,
Give potentates the lie.

Tell men of high condition,
That manage the estate,
Their purpose is ambition,
Their practice only hate:

And if they once reply,
Then give them all the lie.

Tell them that brave it most,
They beg for more by
    spending,
Who, in their greatest cost,
Seek nothing but
    commending.
And if they make reply,
Then give them all the lie.

Tell zeal it wants devotion;
Tell love it is but lust;
Tell time it is but motion;
Tell flesh it is but dust:
And wish them not reply,
For thou must give the lie.

Tell age it daily wasteth;
Tell honor how it alters;
Tell beauty how she blasteth;
Tell favor how it falters:
And as they shall reply,
Give every one the lie.

Tell wit how much it
   wrangles
In tickle points of niceness;
Tell wisdom she entangles
Herself in overwiseness:
And when they do reply,
Straight give them both
   the lie.

Tell arts they have no
   soundness,
But vary by esteeming;
Tell schools they want
   profoundness,
And stand too much on seeming:
If arts and schools reply,
Give arts and schools the lie.

Tell physic of her boldness;
Tell skill it is pretension;
Tell charity of coldness;
Tell law it is contention:
And as they do reply,
So give them still the lie.

Tell faith it's fled the city;
Tell how the country erreth;
Tell manhood shakes off pity
And virtue least preferreth:
And if they do reply,
Spare not to give the lie.

Tell fortune of her blindness;
Tell nature of decay;
Tell friendship of
   unkindness;
Tell justice of delay:
And if they will reply,
Then give them all the lie.

So when thou hast, as I
Commanded thee, done
   blabbing—
Although to give the lie
Deserves no less than stabbing—
Stab at thee he that will,
No stab the soul can kill.

3

Picturing Guiana: Marvels and Monsters
1599

*These graphic materials, which include engravings and a contemporary
map, are meant to demonstrate how* The Discovery of Guiana *fared
once it left Ralegh's hands—or, rather, the hands of his London
printers—and spread an image of Guiana. The* Discovery *was im-
mensely popular outside England, for reasons that may have had little to
do with Ralegh's imperial intentions. In the hands of Continental printers and cartographers, Guiana was a locus of marvels and monsters,
and Ralegh's thrilling report of El Dorado proved an ideal vehicle for*

illustrating such exotica. The non-English variations of the Discovery *commonly took the form of a picture book, the narrative all but subsumed by the fabulous images. The first illustrated editions came from the ateliers of two premier printers, Levinus Hulsius and Theodor de Bry, who were plainly successful in their endeavor. Their books originally appeared in German and Latin, and derivative versions, in various forms and languages, stayed in print for more than a century.*

Figure 5. Customs of the Amazons, *in* Brevis & admiranda descriptio regni Guianae *(Nuremberg: Levinus Hulsius, 1599).*

Note the rather risqué representations of Amazonian lovemaking, along with the symbols (for example, the longbows) of these women's military prowess.

The Huntington Library, Art Collections and Botanical Gardens.

Figure 6. Ewaipanoma, *in* Brevis & admiranda descriptio regni Guianae
(Nuremberg: Levinus Hulsius, 1599).

These "people whose heads appear not above their shoulders" (page 92)
resemble classical *Acephali* (headless men) — wonders of the ancient world no
less than the Renaissance.

The Huntington Library, Art Collections and Botanical Gardens.

Figure 7. Tivitivas, *in* Brevis & admiranda descriptio regni Guianae *(Nuremberg: Levinus Hulsius, 1599).*

The stilt houses of the Warao were inhabited in the rainy season. They are here depicted as full-blown tree houses (in the Atlantic, no less), with scenes of cannibalism off to the right.

The Huntington Library, Art Collections and Botanical Gardens.

Figure 8. How the Nobility of Guiana Would Cover Themselves in Gold When Feasting, *in* Americae pars viii *(Frankfurt a. M.: Widow and Sons of Theodor de Bry, 1599).*

This engraving shows the central practice of "el Dorado"—namely, the use of gold as body ornament among Guiana's elite. De Bry has endowed the central figure with classical features—sculpted musculature and *contrapposto* (slightly twisted) pose—which allies these "noble" Indians with ancient statuary and with Renaissance humanist culture.

The Huntington Library, Art Collections and Botanical Gardens.

Figure 9. How Ralegh Made Alliance with the King of Arromaia, *in Americae pars viii (Frankfurt a. M.: Widow and Sons of Theodor de Bry, 1599).*

This scene of Ralegh's meeting with Toparimaca (page 82) serves two purposes. It shows the alliance of the English and local Indians, which would potentially counter Spanish power in America, and it depicts the ample generosity of the Indians, who offer their rich products (including maize). Note de Bry's subtle expression of doubt, however, in the form of the musketeer at the ready on the right and the leftmost soldier, who glances toward the armed Indians in the rear.

The Huntington Library, Art Collections and Botanical Gardens.

Figure 10. Their Ceremonies for the Dead *in* Americae pars viii *(Frankfurt a. M.: Widow and Sons of Theodor de Bry, 1599)*.

This display of ancestral bones—technically, a process of secondary burial—would have been seen by Europeans as a marvel, as would the Warao practice of tree dwelling, depicted in the background (see Figure 7).

The Huntington Library, Art Collections and Botanical Gardens.

Opposite: **Figure 11.** Guiana, *ca. 1599, Jodocus Hondius.*

This map was printed in de Bry's editions of Ralegh's text and as a separate sheet map, and it circulated widely and in multiple languages. Hondius was an important Flemish engraver and cartographer who, like de Bry, had no first-hand experience of America. Note the array of wonders—an armadillo, various large cats (pumas?), the Ewaipanoma—that inhabit this "gold-rich" empire.

The Huntington Library, Art Collections and Botanical Gardens.

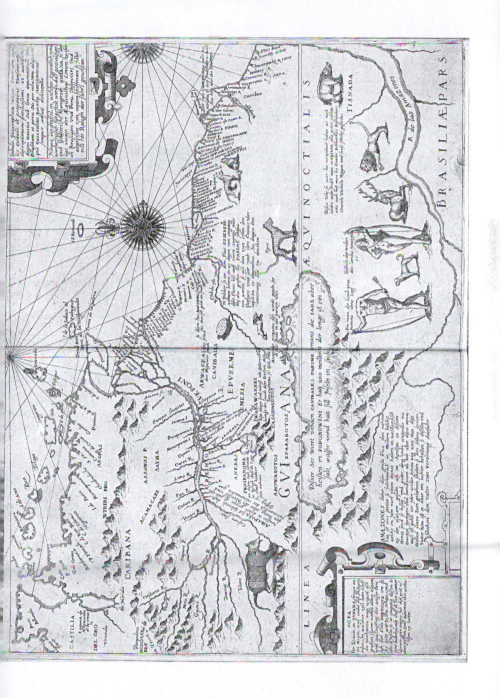

4

The Travels of Sir John Mandeville

ca. 1356

Medieval Europe obtained its knowledge of the exotic world mostly from books, and the geography book most Europeans read (or heard) may well have been The Travels of Sir John Mandeville. *Mandeville, who is otherwise unknown (and likely a pseudonym), claimed to have circled the known world as a pilgrim, observing the state of global Christianity. In fact, his book offered the most complete—and entertaining—roster of marvels and monsters, intermixing along the way what passed back then for sober ethnography. "Back then" begins in the mid-fourteenth century, when manuscripts of the* Travels *first circulated, yet the text persisted well into the age of print. Ralegh cites Mandeville directly and surely owned a copy of his book. Ralegh was keen to confirm the presence in Guiana of the Ewaipanoma (headless men) of which Mandeville wrote, and he may have had Mandeville in mind when he described the Amazons (warrior women) and other unusual inhabitants of the tropics. The passages excerpted here contain fairly typical descriptions of Amazonian women and other curious creatures of Europe's exotic world.*

Next to Chaldea is the land of Amazoun [the Amazons], which we call the Maiden Land or the Land of Women; no man lives there, only women. This is not because, as some say, no man can live there, but because the women will not allow men to rule the kingdom. There was once a king in that land called Colopheus, and there were once men living there as they do elsewhere. It so happened that this king went to war with the King of Scythia, and was slain with all his great men in battle with his enemy. And when the Queen and the other ladies of that land heard the news that the King and the lords were slain, they marshalled themselves with one accord and armed themselves well. They took a great army of women and slaughtered all the men left among them. And since that time they will never let a man

The Travels of Sir John Mandeville, trans. and ed. C. W. R. D. Moseley (Harmondsworth: Penguin, 1983), 116–18, 134–35.

live with them more than seven days, nor will they allow a boy child to be brought up among them. But when they want to have the company of man, they go to that side of their country where their lovers live, stay with them eight or nine days and then go home again. If any of them bears a child and it is a son, they keep it until it can speak and walk and eat by itself and then they send it to the father—or they kill it. If they have a girl child, they cut off one of her breasts and cauterize it; in the case of a woman of great estate, the left one, so that she can carry her shield better, and, in one of low degree, they cut off the right, so that it will not hinder them shooting—for they know very well the skill of archery. There is always a queen to rule that land, and they all obey her. This queen is always chosen by election, for they choose the woman who is the best fighter. These women are noble and wise warriors; and therefore kings of neighbouring realms hire them to help them in their wars. This land of the Amazons is an island, surrounded by water, except at two points where there are two ways in. Beyond the water live their lovers to whom they go when it pleases them to have bodily pleasure with them. . . .

On the other side of Chaldea, to the south, is the land of Ethiopia, . . . [where] all the rivers are so turbid and so salt because of the excessive heat of the sun that no one dare use them. The people of that country very easily get drunk; they have little appetite for their food, and commonly have diarrhoea. They live only a short time. In that land, too, there are people of different shapes. There are some who have only one foot, and yet they run so fast on that one foot that it is a marvel to see them. That foot is so big that it will cover and shade all the body from the sun. In Ethiopia are young children whose hair is white, and as they grow old, their hair gets black. . . .

And from this country you go via many others in the sea to one called Melk [Malacca?]. There are wicked and cruel folk there too. For they have no delight or pleasure in anything except slaughtering people to drink their blood. And the man who can kill the greatest number of men is the most respected and worthiest among them. There is no drink they like so much as man's blood, and they call it God. If there is any quarrel among them, no full agreement can be made until each has drunk the other's blood; and in the same way relationships are sealed between them. Agreements and relationships among them are not valid unless made in this way.

From here one goes to another isle, called Tracota, where the people are like animals lacking reason. They live in caves, for they do not have the intelligence to build houses; and when they see a stranger passing through the country, they run and hide in their caves. They eat snakes, and do not speak, but hiss to one another like adders. They care nothing for gold, silver, or other worldly goods, only for one precious stone which has sixty colours. It is called traconite after the country. They love this stone very much indeed, even though they do not know its properties; they desire it simply for its beauty.

Thence one travels by sea to another land, called Natumeran [Nicobar islands]. It is a large and fair island, whose circuit is nearly a thousand miles. Men and women of that isle have heads like dogs, and they are called Cynocephales. These people, despite their shape, are fully reasonable and intelligent. They worship an ox as their god. Each one of them carries an ox made of gold or silver on his brow, as a token that they love their god well. They go quite naked except for a little cloth round their privy parts. They are big in stature and good warriors; they carry a large shield, which covers all their body, and a long spear in their hand, and dressed in this way they go boldly against their enemies. If they capture any man in battle, they eat him. The King of that land is a great and mighty lord, rich, and very devout according to his creed. He has round his neck a cord of silk on which are three hundred precious stones [orient pearls], like our rosary of amber. And just as we say our *Pater Noster* and *Aue Maria* by telling our beads, just so the King says each day on his beads three hundred prayers to his god, before he eats. He wears a splendid ruby round his neck, which is nearly a foot long and five fingers broad. They give him this ruby when they make him King, to carry in his hand, and so he rides round the city and they all make obeisance to him. After that he always wears it round his neck, for if he did not he would be King no longer.

5

BARTOLOMÉ DE LAS CASAS

A Short Account of the Destruction of the Indies

1552

Las Casas's Brevíssima relación *(Short Account), first published in 1552, was perhaps the single most influential work on America printed in early modern Europe. It went through scores of editions, in all major European languages (English edition, 1583), and it was reprinted as late as 1898, during the Spanish-American War. Ralegh surely knew of it — he cites it directly in "Of the Voyage for Guiana" (Document 6) — and he was surely influenced by Las Casas's fiery rhetoric and arguments. The latter might be described as explicitly pro-Indian and implicitly anti-Spanish. A Dominican friar, Las Casas lived for years in America and witnessed countless atrocities committed against the Indians. He not only exposed the "cruelties" of the Conquista, but he also laid the blame on the Spanish, who had failed their religious and moral charge in America. In the passages excerpted here, Las Casas details those "tyrannies" committed in the region near Guiana, some of which Ralegh would himself recount. Here and elsewhere in the tract, Las Casas asserts that the Indians yearned to be freed from the Spanish yoke, a case Ralegh would vigorously embrace in his own writings on America.*

The whole of the area lying between the Paria and the Gulf of Venezuela, a distance of some two hundred leagues, has been the scene of wholesale destruction wrought upon the indigenous people by Spanish adventurers who have attacked them, taking as many as possible alive to sell as slaves. Often they have achieved this by deception, offering the people friendship and safe conduct and then going back on their word in a totally shameless fashion, even after the people have welcomed them into their homes as though they were long-lost brothers and done everything they possibly can for them. It would be impossible to compile a detailed and accurate record of every instance

Bartolomé de Las Casas, *A Short Account of the Destruction of the Indies*, trans. Nigel Griffin, introduction by Anthony Pagden (New York: Penguin, 1992), 88–93, 125–26.

of injustice, insult, harassment and outrage suffered by the people of the coast at the hands of the Spanish between 1510 and now, and I shall describe only two or three incidents as examples of countless such ugly atrocities, each and every one of them sufficient to earn the perpetrators the everlasting torment of Hellfire.

The people who live on the island of Trinidad, which is both larger and more fertile than Sicily and lies just off the mainland close by Paria, are as good and virtuous as any to be found anywhere in the New World. In 1516, one of these adventurers made his way there with sixty or seventy men experienced in the ways of robbery and announced that he and his men were coming to settle on the island and to live alongside the native people. The locals welcomed them as though they were their own flesh and blood, both the chief and the people dancing attendance upon them, showing every sign of joy and affection, and bringing them every single day twice as much food as they could possibly eat. Indeed, the indigenous peoples of the New World are by nature extremely generous and, in their rush to provide the Spanish with more than they need, often hand over everything they possess. They built a large wooden house big enough for all the members of the Spanish expedition to live in, since the Spaniards insisted on being quartered together in order that they might carry out the plan they had hatched. Once the wooden framework of the house was complete, work began on thatching the structure. As soon as the walls were finished to more than twice the height of a man and those inside the building could no longer see what was going on out-side, the Spanish made a great pretence of wanting to finish the job as quickly as possible and packed a very large number of men inside the building. They then took their arms and deployed themselves around the outside of the house to seal off all the exits, and also stationed a number of men inside the building itself. Those inside then drew their swords and instructed the naked and defenceless natives to stand per-fectly still, threatening to kill them if they did not. They next began to tie them up, while those that tried to escape were hacked to pieces by the guards stationed outside. A few did manage to get away, although some were wounded in the process, and regrouped in another build-ing, joining forces with those locals who had not been in the new house during the attack. Here they set about defending themselves as best they could with bows and arrows. There were between a hundred and two hundred of them, but the Spanish posted men on the doors to prevent any escape and then set fire to the building, burning them alive, before making for their ship, taking with them a prize consisting of the one hundred and eighty to two hundred men they had seized and bound at the outset and, setting sail for Puerto Rico, they sold half of the consignment there as slaves before sailing on to Hispaniola where they sold the rest. . . .

On another occasion, the Dominicans, our own Order, decided to mount a mission to bring the Word of Christ to the peoples of the New World because they were ignorant of the truth and were accordingly (and still are) in mortal danger of being denied the Life Everlasting. It was decided to send among them a monk, a man of great virtue and holiness and fully versed in theology, and he was to have a lay brother as his companion. The idea was that they should get to know the lie of the land and make contact with local people with a view to deciding where best to establish monasteries. The people received them as angels from Heaven, listening with rapt attention and great emotion and joy to what they had to say, even though this had to be conveyed by sign and gesture as the Dominicans did not speak the local language. After the ship which had brought the missionaries had sailed away another vessel arrived. The Dominicans were not aware of it at the time, but the Spaniards invited the local chief on board this vessel together with a hundred of his men, ostensibly for a party. This local chief, who was known as Alonso (presumably a name given him by the Spaniards or by the missionaries, local people being very keen to acquire a Christian name and often asking for one even before they are taught the rudiments of Christianity necessary for baptism), would not normally have trusted such an invitation but he was tricked into a false sense of security by the presence of the Dominicans, believing that the Spaniards would not do him any harm all the time the missionaries were there. He, his wife and seventeen others went on board, but no sooner had they done so than the ship set sail for Hispaniola where the hostages were sold into slavery. The people, seeing their chief and his wife carried off in this manner, were minded to execute the missionaries in return, and the missionaries themselves were mortified at the wickedness shown by the Spanish, for they would have died rather than countenance such treachery, especially as they sensed it would prove a real obstacle to the conversion of the people. They did their best to mollify them, assuring them that they would send word to Hispaniola by the first available vessel and would contrive to ensure the safe return of the chief and those who were with him. As God would have it, a vessel did arrive and with it an opportunity to confirm the perfidy of those in authority throughout the region. For the Dominicans duly wrote to their fellow-missionaries on

Hispaniola, protesting repeatedly about this treachery, only for it soon to become plain that the magistrates there had no intention of investigating the case because they had themselves received a number of the slaves taken in this evil and criminal fashion. . . .

Another incident occurred in this same area, at Codera Point, where stood a town whose chief was known as Higoroto, which was either the chief's own name or possibly a title given to all the lords in the area in question. The chief himself was a goodly man and his people so virtuous that a Spaniard putting in there could be sure to find food and rest, and an opportunity to relax and recuperate. Indeed, many Spaniards who fetched up there, dropping from exhaustion and hunger in their headlong rush to escape from other parts of the country that they had made too hot for themselves by their atrocities and excesses, and whom he could have quietly despatched without anyone being any the wiser, were instead given food and safe passage to Margarita Island where there was a Christian garrison. In short, the town of Higueroto was known to all the Europeans as every man's hostel and every man's home. The local people had no apparent reason to be on their guard against anybody and, because of this, one Spanish adventurer decided they would be easy game. He sailed in and issued a general invitation for the locals to come aboard his ship, which was something they were used to doing when Spanish vessels were in port. With many of them—men, women and children—safely on board, he set sail for Puerto Rico, where he sold them all into slavery. When I myself arrived in Puerto Rico, I met this Spanish captain and learned in detail of what he had done. He was responsible for the destruction of the entire town, an abomination which gave rise to great consternation among the Spanish adventurers operating in the area, all of whom looked upon it as a safe refuge and a home from home.

I repeat that many similar atrocities and countless acts of wickedness will here pass unremarked, even though they continue unabated to the present day.

From what was once the heavily populated coastal area of the Paria Peninsula, over two million souls have been kidnapped and taken to the islands of Hispaniola and Puerto Rico to be sent down the mines or put to other work. There, as did those of whom we spoke earlier, they perished in droves. It is a heartrending sight to travel along that coast, once so fertile and so populous, and to see it as it is today, totally abandoned and left to go to rack and ruin.

It is a fact beyond dispute that whenever one of these vessels sets sail, loaded to the gunwales with natives who have been rounded up and forcibly embarked, at least a third of the poor wretches perish during the voyage and are thrown overboard, and one has also to remember that many are killed before they ever get as far as the ships. The reason the death-toll is so high is that, in order to maximize profits, the men who finance these slave-fleets arrange for the vessels to carry nothing in the way of victuals except a basic minimum for the crew and so there is hardly any food or water for the poor prisoners who, as a consequence, perish from thirst and hunger and are consigned to a watery grave. One witness told me personally that, on a voyage from the Bahamas, where many natives had been rounded up, to Hispaniola, a distance of sixty or seventy leagues, one vessel, which was navigating without a compass and with no chart of the region, kept its course only by reference to the string of dead bodies wallowing in its wake.

Later, the spectacle of these poor creatures disembarked on the island where they are to be sold is enough to break the heart of anyone with a spark of human feeling. They are naked, and so weakened by hunger that many—old and young alike, men and women—simply drop where they stand. Then they are split up into groups of between ten and twenty, like so many sheep being driven to market: a parent is parted from a child, a woman from her husband; and lots are cast as a way of apportioning the little flocks between the wretched *armadores* (the individuals who originally pooled resources to charter the two or three vessels that make up the slave convoy) and those who actually sailed to the native villages and took part in the round-up itself. If a man finds himself allotted a flock in which there is an old man or in which someone is sickly, his response is normally: "To the Devil with this old man. Why make me take him? I suppose you want me to bury him? Why should I take this sickly one? Am I to waste my substance on curing him?" Reactions like these serve to give some idea of what the Spanish think of the native people, and how closely they obey that commandment to love one's neighbour that underpins the Law and the books of the Prophets. . . .

I should like now to say no more—until, that is, fresh reports arrive of worse evils (if such there could be) or until I am in a position to return to the region to see matters for myself. For forty-two years now, these matters have been constantly before my eyes and on my mind, and I can honestly say, as God is my witness, that I have solid grounds for believing that the depredations, the harm, the destruction, the depopulation, the atrocities and massacres, the horrible cruelty and barbarism, the violence, the injustice, the plunder and the whole-sale murder that all these territories have witnessed and their people suffered (and still suffer) are on such a scale that what I have here been able to relate is no more than a thousandth part of the reality of what has been taking place and continues to take place.

Recognition of the truth will make the reader more compassionate towards the sufferings and the predicament of these poor innocent peoples and oblige him to adopt an even more stern and censorious attitude towards the abominable greed, ambition and brutality of their Spanish oppressors; and no Christian who reads this should be in any doubt, even for a moment, that there has ever been a single instance, from the date of the discovery of the New World down to the present, when the indigenous people have committed even the slightest offence against the Europeans without due provocation, and that it has been the wicked plunder and the treachery of the Europeans that have given rise to all the evils we have described. Indeed, the natives believed the Europeans immortal and to be descended from the heavens and they welcomed them as such, at least until the actions of these celestial beings finally revealed what sort of creatures they were and what it was they were after.

6

SIR WALTER RALEGH

Of the Voyage for Guiana

ca. 1596

This brief overview of the Guiana project was written by or for Ralegh (the unsigned manuscript appears to be in Ralegh's hand yet it has also been ascribed to Lawrence Keymis and to Thomas Harriot). Unlike the Discovery, *however, it was never published and should be read as an internal "court" document, a policy paper intended for the queen's closest*

This excerpt is a modernized version of the 1596 text, Sir Walter Ralegh, *The Discoverie of the Large and Bewtiful Empyre of Guiana*, ed. V. T. Harlow (London: Argonaut Press, 1928), 138–49.

advisers. The author expresses in remarkably direct language the rationale for the voyage and the expected payoff of colonization; he prioritizes. Moreover, in contrast to the printed Discovery, *which personalizes the voyage and emphasizes the courtier's relationship with the queen, this document reads briskly and efficiently, keeping the larger geopolitical agenda front and center. This agenda might be neatly summarized as ideological, economic, and imperial (with a fair degree of overlap). The author lists, above all, the spiritual gains of the enterprise—the care for the Indians' souls—which he couples with the broader, global fight against Spanish "tyranny," understood to encompass both Habsburg imperialism and Roman Catholic expansionism. The passage excerpted here contains an exceptionally vivid description of (purported) Spanish abuses in America, which suggests that such arguments—and rhetoric— were seen as effective in the queen's court no less than in the court of public opinion.*

Note that the document continues for several more pages explicating more precisely how the Guiana enterprise might proceed (the selection excerpted having explained why*). This entails a fascinating argument for colonization "according to our Christian profession"—namely, a more moral approach to empire than that taken by Catholic Spain, which rationalized its military conquests based on a papal bull of 1494.*

Touching the voyage for Guiana, it is to be considered first, whether it [is] to be undertaken; secondly, the manner of subduing it; and lastly, the means how to subdue it, and annex it to the Crown Imperial of the Realm of England.

That it is to be undertaken will appear, if it be proved to be (1) honorable, (2) profitable, (3) necessary, (4) and with no great charge, or difficulty accomplished.

1. It is honorable, both for that by this means infinite numbers of souls may be brought from their idolatry, bloody sacrifices, ignorance, and incivility to the worshipping of the true God aright[1] to civil conversation. And also their bodies freed from the intolerable tyranny of the Spaniards, whereunto they are already or likely in short space to be subjected, unless her excellent Majesty or some other Christian prince do speedily assist and afterward protect them in their just defensive wars against the violence of usurpers. Which, if it please her

---

[1]Rightly or correctly; straightaway.

highness to undertake, besides that presently it will stop the mouths of the Romish Catholics, who vaunt of their great adventures for the propagation of the gospel, it will add great increase of honor to the memory of her Majesty's name upon earth to all posterity and in the end be rewarded with an excellent starlike splendency in the heavens, which is reserved for them that turn many unto righteousness as the Prophet speaketh.

2. Likewise it is profitable, for hereby the Queen's dominions may be exceedingly enlarged, and this Realm inestimably enriched, with precious stones, gold, silver, pearl, and other commodities which those countries yield, and (God giving good success to the voyage) an entrance made thereby to many other Empires (which happily may prove as rich as this), and it may be to Peru itself and other kingdoms of which the Spaniards be now possessed, in those parts and elsewhere.

3. Lastly, the necessity of attempting Guiana in regard of our own security (albeit no profit should redound thereby to the Indians, or to ourselves directly from those countries) ought greatly to weigh with us. For if the Spaniards, by the treasure of those kingdoms which he hath already, be able to trouble the better part of Christendom, what would he do if he were once established in Guiana, which is thought to be more rich than all other lands which he enjoyeth either in the East or West Indies. Whereas if her Majesty were seized of it, he might be so kept occupied in those provinces that he would not hastily threaten us with any more of his invincible navies.

But although this voyage were never so honorable, profitable, or necessary for our estate to be undertaken, yet if we had not some possibility for the effecting of our purpose, it were more meet to strengthen ourselves at home, than to weaken our forces in seeking to annoy our enemy abroad. But such opportunity and so many encouragements do now offer themselves unto her highness that (I suppose) there is no prince in the world but he would greatly strain himself, rather than to omit the advantage of such a booty. Among others, these inducements are to be weighed.

1. The Borderers, who are said to be naturals, and to whom only the Empire of Guiana doth of right appertain,[2] are already prepared to join with us, having submitted themselves to the Queen's protection

[2]Belong.

both against the Spaniards and Emperor of Guiana who usurpeth upon them.

2. The Spaniards, for their oppressions and usurpations, are detested and feared both by the Guianians and borderers: by the former, because the Spaniards forced them to fly from their own country of Peru; and by the latter, by experience of the Spanish dealing towards themselves and their adjoining neighbors. So as it is reported none do assist them save the Arwacans, a vagabond, poor, and small people. But it is likely that all the countries of the continent who are not yet enthralled to the Spaniards and have heard of their outrage and especially the Amazones in regard of their sex, will be ready to aid her Majesty against the Spaniards.

3. The voyage is short, being but 6 weeks sailing from England and the like back again, which may so be contrived as going, abiding,[3] and returning we may bestow a whole year without any winter at all by the way, no lee shore, no sands, or enemy's coast.

4. No charge but only at the first setting forth, which need not be great, especially if the course laid down in this treatise of some such like be taken, considering the country yieldeth store of corn, beasts, fowl, fish, and fruit for victuals, and steel and copper for the making of armor and ordinance,[4] and among the Amapagotos and Caracas horses may be had and in short time manned for our service in the wars.

5. It is thought the passage to it may be easily fortified by sea and the country by nature is defensed by land with mountains and multitude of nations, that it is impossible in manner by land to be evicted, being once attained by us.

6. Though we are not greatly to rely upon prophecies, yet if it were found in Peru (as Don Antonio de Berreo told Sir Walter Ralegh) among other prophecies that from Inglatiera the Inca should be restored to Peru, it may fall out to be true (as many of their prophecies did both in Mexico and Peru, which indeed foreshewed the alteration of those Empires), at least the prophecy will greatly daunt the Spaniards and make them afraid of the worst event in these employments.

7. If it be remembered how the Spaniards have, without just title or any wrong at all done to them by the harmless Indians, forcibly invaded and wrongfully detained their countries about 100 years, com-

---

[3] Remaining, staying.
[4] Ordnance: military materials, especially artillery and heavy firearms.

mitting barbarous and exquisite massacres to the destruction of whole nations of people (arising by estimation of some of account[5] among them and acquainted with their proceedings in some few years to the number of 20 millions of reasonable creatures made to the image of God and less harmful than the Spaniards themselves),[6] whereby more fruitful land was laid waste and depopulated than is in all Europe and some part of Asia, in revenge whereof their own religious men do make account that the just God in judgment will one day horribly chasten and peradventure[7] wholly subvert and root out the Spanish nation from the world. Again if it be noted that the Spaniards have above 20 several times in vain sought the conquest of Guiana, and that it doth by the providence of the Almighty now (as it were) prostrate herself before her Majesty's feet the most potent enemy that the Spaniards hath, not only entreating but by unvaluable offers and unanswerable reasons alluring, even urging and forcing her highness to accept it under her allegiance, who would not be persuaded that now at length the great judge of the world hath heard the sighs, groans, lamentations, tears, and blood of so many millions of innocent men, women, and children afflicted, robbed, reviled, branded with hot irons, roasted, dismembered, mangled, stabbed, whipped, racked, scalded with hot oil, suet,[8] and hog's grease, put to the strappado,[9] ripped alive, beheaded in sport, drowned, dashed against the rocks, famished, devoured by mastiffs, burned, and by infinite cruelties consumed, and purposeth to scourge and plague that cursed nation, and to take the yoke of servitude from that distressed people, as free by nature as any Christian. In comtemplation of all which things, who would not be encouraged to proceed in this voyage, having in a manner none other enemies but these Spaniards, abhorred of God and man, being provoked by so many allurements, occasions, reasons, and opportunities, in a most just cause, the safety of our dread sovereign, of ourselves, and of a great part of the Christian world thereupon depending.

---

[5]Some who can be trusted; reliable authorities.
[6]This was the estimate of Las Casas (see Document 5).
[7]Perhaps; possibly.
[8]Animal fat used in cooking and candle making.
[9]A form of torture in which the victim's hands were tied behind his or her back and fastened to a pulley. The victim was then lifted up from the ground and let down halfway, stopping with a jerk to maximize the pain.

THOMAS HARRIOT

A Brief and True Report
of the New Found Land of Virginia
1588

A close associate of Ralegh, Thomas Harriot wrote his True Report *shortly after participating in the Roanoke voyages of 1584–1587. It originally appeared in 1588 but earned even greater popularity in an illustrated form published by de Bry in 1590. Harriot, who would go on to become a highly regarded mathematician and astronomer, served the expedition at Ralegh's behest as navigator and all-around "scientist." It is in the latter capacity that he compiled notes for the* True Report: *field observations of the land, its agricultural promise, and its native inhabitants. In this excerpt, Harriot describes the Carolina Algonquians in relatively straightforward and admiring terms. This may reflect the promotional nature of the tract—Harriot and Ralegh hoped to win support for their overseas efforts—yet it is worth noting all the same England's more open and optimistic approach to the indigenous peoples of America at this early stage in their colonial enterprise. Ralegh would record his impressions of the Guianans just a few years later, and one detects a similar quality of open inquisitiveness in both the patron (Ralegh) and his client (Harriot).*

Of the Nature and Manners of the People

It resteth I speak a word or two of the natural inhabitants, their natures and manners, leaving large discourse thereof until time more convenient hereafter; now only so far forth as that you may know how that they, in respect of troubling our inhabiting and planting, are not to be feared, but that they shall have cause both to fear and love us, that shall inhabit with them.

Thomas Harriot, *A Briefe and True Report of the New Found Land of Virginia* (London: [R. Robinson], 1588), sig. Ev–F2v.

They are a people clothed with loose mantles made of deer skins, and aprons of the same round about their middles, all else naked, of such a difference of statures only as we in England, having no edge tools or weapons of iron or steel to offend us withal, neither know they how to make any. Those weapons that they have are only bows made of witch hazel and arrows of reeds, flat edged truncheons also of wood about a yard long, neither have they any thing to defend themselves but targets[1] made of barks, and some armors made of sticks wickered together with thread.

Their towns are but small, and near the sea coast but few, some containing but ten or twelve houses; some 20. The greatest that we have seen hath been but of 30 houses. If they be walled, it is only done with barks of trees made fast to stakes, or else with poles only fixed upright, and close one by another.

Their houses are made of small poles, made fast at the tops in round form after the manner as is used in many arbories in our gardens of England, in most towns covered with barks, and in some with artificial mats made of long rushes, from the tops of the houses down to the ground. The length of them is commonly double to the breadth; in some places they are but 12 and 16 yards long, and in other some we have seen of four and twenty.

In some places of the country, one only town belongeth to the government of a Wiroans[2] or chief Lord, in other some two or three, in some six, eight, and more. The greatest Wiroans that yet we had dealing with had but eighteen towns in his government, and able to make not above seven or eight hundred fighting men at the most. The language of every government is different from any other, and the further they are distant, the greater is the difference.

Their manner of wars amongst themselves is either by sudden surprising one another, most commonly about the dawning of the day or moonlight, or else by ambushes, or some subtle devices. Set battles are very rare, except it fall out where there are many trees, where either part may have some hope of defence, after the delivery of every arrow, in leaping behind some or other.

If there fall out any wars between us and them, what their fight is likely to be, we having advantages against them so many manner of ways, as by our discipline, our strange weapons and devices else, especially Ordinance[3] great and small, it may easily be imagined. By

---

[1] Light, round shields.
[2] A chief of the Virginia Indians.
[3] Mode of battle or display of military force.

the experience we have had in some places, the turning up of their heels against us in running away was their best defence.

In respect of us they are a people poor, and for want of skill and judgement in the knowledge and use of our things do esteem our trifles before things of greater value. Notwithstanding, in their proper manner (considering the want of such means as we have), they seem very ingenious. For although they have no such tools, nor any such crafts, Sciences and Arts as we, yet in those things they do they shew excellence of wit. And by how much they upon due consideration shall find our manner of knowledges and crafts to exceed theirs in perfection, and speed for doing or execution, by so much the more is it probable that they should desire our friendship and love, and have the greater respect for pleasing and obeying us. Whereby may be hoped, if means of good government be used, that they may in short time be brought to civility, and the embracing of true Religion.

Some religion they have already, which although it be far from the truth, yet being as it is, there is hope it may be the easier and sooner reformed.

They believe that there are many gods, which they call Mantoac, but of different sorts and degrees, one only chief and great God, which hath been from all eternity. Who, as they affirm, when he purposed to make the world, made first other gods of a principal order to be as means and instruments to be used in the creation and government to follow, and after the sun, moon, and stars as petty gods, and the instruments of the other order more principal. First (they say) were made waters, out of which by the gods was made all diversity of creatures that are visible or invisible.

For mankind they say a woman was made first, which by the working of one of the gods, conceived and brought forth children; and in such sort they say they had their beginning. But how many years or ages have passed since, they say they can make no relation, having no letters nor other such means as we to keep records of the particularities of times past, but only tradition from father to son.

They think that all the gods are of human shape, and therefore they represent them by images in the forms of men, which they call Kewasowok, one alone is called Kewas; them they place in houses appropriate or temples, which they call Machicomuck, where they worship, pray, sing, and make many times offering unto them. In some Machicomuck we have seen but one Kewas, in some two, and in other some three. The common sort think them to be also gods.

They believe also the immortality of the soul, that after this life as soon as the soul is departed from the body, according to the works it hath done, it is either carried to heaven the habitacle[4] of gods, there to enjoy perpetual bliss and happiness, or else to a great pit or hole, which they think to be in the furthest parts of their part of the world toward the sunset, there to burn continually: the place they call Popogusso.

For the confirmation of this opinion, they told me two stories of two men that had been lately dead and revived again. The one happened but few years before our coming into the country, of a wicked man, which having been dead and buried, the next day the earth of the grave being seen to move, was taken up again, who made declaration where his soul had been, that is to say, very near entering into Popogusso, had not one of the gods saved him, and gave him leave to return again, and teach his friends what they should do to avoid that terrible place of torment. The other happened in the same year we were there, but in a town that was 60 miles from us, and it was told me for strange news, that one being dead, buried, and taken up again as the first, shewed that although his body had lain dead in the grave, yet his soul was alive, and had travailed[5] far in a long broad way, on both sides whereof grew most delicate and pleasant trees, bearing more rare and excellent fruits, than ever he had seen before, or was able to express, and at length came to most brave and fair houses, near which he met his father that had been dead before, who gave him great charge to go back again, and shew his friends what good they were to do to enjoy the pleasures of that place, which when he had done he should after come again.

What subtlety soever be in the Wiroances and priests, this opinion worketh so much in many of the common and simple sort of people, that it maketh them have great respect to their governours, and also great care what they do to avoid torment after death, and to enjoy bliss, although notwithstanding there is punishment ordained for male-factours, as stealers, whoremongers, and other sorts of wicked doers, some punished with death, some with forfeitures,[6] some with beating, according to the greatness of the facts.

And this is the sum of their religion, which I learned by having special familiarity with some of their priests. Wherein they were not so sure grounded, nor gave such credit to their traditions and stories, but through conversing with us they were brought into great doubts of

---

[4]Dwelling place.
[5]Traveled.
[6]Deprivation of an estate after committing a crime.

their own, and no small admiration of ours, with earnest desire in many to learn more than we had means for want of perfect utterance in their language to express.

Most things they saw with us as mathematical instruments, sea compasses, the virtue of the lodestone[7] in drawing iron, a perspective glass[8] whereby was showed many strange sights, burning glasses,[9] wild fireworks, guns, hooks, writing and reading, springclocks that seem to go of themselves and many other things that we had were so strange unto them, and so far exceeded their capacities to comprehend the reason and means how they should be made and done, that they thought they were rather the works of gods than of men, or at the leastwise they had been given and taught us of the gods. Which made many of them to have such opinion of us, as that if they knew not the truth of God and Religion already, it was rather to be had from us whom God so specially loved, than from a people that were so simple, as they found themselves to be in comparison of us. Whereupon greater credit was given unto that we spake of concerning such matters.

Many times and in every town where I came, according as I was able, I made declaration of the contents of the Bible, that therein was set forth the true and only God, and his mighty works, that therein was contained the true doctrine of salvation through Christ, with many particularities of miracles and chief points of religion, as I was able then to utter, and thought fit for the time. And although I told them the book materially and of itself was not of any such virtue, as I thought they did conceive, but only the doctrine therein contained; yet would many be glad to touch it, to embrace it, to kiss it, to hold it to their breasts and heads, and stroke over all their body with it, to shew their hungry desire of that knowledge which was spoken of.

The Wiroans with whom we dwelt, called Wingina, and many of his people would be glad many times to be with us at our prayers, and many times call upon us both in his own town, as also in others whither he sometimes accompanied us, to pray and sing Psalms, hoping thereby to be partaker of the same effects which we by that means also expected.

Twice this Wiroans was so grievously sick that he was like to die,

[7]Magnetic oxide of iron; that is, a magnet attracting iron.
[8]Optical instrument for looking through; also, a device commonly made with mirrors for producing optical effects.
[9]Lens or mirror used to concentrate the rays of the sun in order to start a fire.

and as he lay languishing, doubting of any help by his own priests, and thinking he was in such danger for offending us and thereby our God, sent for some of us to pray and be a means to our God that it would please him either that he might live, or after death dwell with him in bliss. So likewise were the requests of many others in the like case.

On a time also when their corn began to wither by reason of a drought which happened extraordinarily, fearing that it had come to pass by reason that in some thing they had displeased us, many would come to us and desire us to pray to our God of England, that he would preserve their corn, promising that when it was ripe we also should be partakers of the fruit.

There could at no time happen any strange sickness, losses, hurts, or any other cross unto them, but that they would impute to us the cause or means thereof, for offending or not pleasing us. One other rare and strange accident, leaving others, will I mention before I end, which moved the whole country that either knew or heard of us, to have us in wonderful admiration.

There was no town where we had any subtle device practiced against us, we leaving it unpunished or not revenged (because we sought by all means possible to win them by gentleness) but that within a few days after our departure from every such town, the people began to die very fast, and many in short space, in some towns about twenty, in some forty, and in one six score, which in truth was very many in respect of their numbers. This happened in no place that we could learn, but where we had been, where they used some practice against us, and after such time. The disease also was so strange, that they neither knew what it was, nor how to cure it, the like by report of the oldest men in the country never happened before, time out of mind: a thing specially observed by us, as also by the natural inhabitants themselves. Insomuch that when some of the inhabitants which were our friends, and especially the Wiroans Wingina, had observed such effects in four or five towns to follow their wicked practices, they were persuaded that it was the work of our God through our means, and that we by him might kill and slay whom we would without weapons and not come near them. And thereupon when it had happened that they had understanding that any of their enemies had abused us in our journeys, hearing that we had wrought no revenge with our weapons and fearing upon some cause the matter should so rest, did come and entreat us that we would be a means to our God that they as others that had dealt ill with us might in like sort die, alleging how much it would be for our credit and profit, as also theirs, and hoping furthermore that we would do so much at their requests in respect of the friendship we professed them.

Whose entreaties, although we shewed that they were ungodly, affirming that our God would not subject himself to any such prayers and requests of men—that indeed all things have been and were to be done according to his good pleasure as he had ordained—and that we to shew ourselves his true servants ought rather to make petition for the contrary, that they with them might live together with us, be made partakers of his truth, and serve him in rightousness, but notwithstanding in such sort, that we refer that, as all other things, to be done according to his divine will and pleasure, and as by his wisdom he had ordained to be best.

Yet because the effect fell out so suddenly and shortly after according to their desires, they thought nevertheless it came to pass by our means, and that we in using such speeches unto them did but dissemble the matter, and therefore came unto us to give us thanks in their manner, that although we satisfied them not in promise, yet in deeds and effect we had fulfilled their desires.

This marvellous accident in all the country wrought so strange opinions of us, that some people could not tell whether to think us gods or men, and the rather because that all the space of their sickness, there was no man of ours known to die, or that was especially sick. They noted also that we had no women amongst us, neither that we did care for any of theirs.

Some therefore were of opinion that we were not born of women, and therefore not mortal, but that we were men of an old generation many years past, then risen again to immortality.

Some would likewise seem to prophesy that there were more of our generation yet to come to kill theirs and take their places, as some thought the purpose was, by that which was already done. Those that were immediately to come after us they imagined to be in the air, yet invisible and without bodies, and that they by our entreaty and for the love of us, did make the people to die in that sort as they did, by shooting invisible bullets into them.

To confirm this opinion, their physicians (to excuse their ignorance in curing the disease) would not be ashamed to say, but earnestly make the simple people believe, that the strings of blood that they sucked out of the sick bodies were the strings wherewithal the invisible bullets were tied and cast. Some also thought that we shot them ourselves out of our pieces from the place where we dwelt and killed the people in any town that had offended us, as we listed,[10] how far distant from us soever it were. And other some said, that it was the special work of God for our sakes, as we ourselves have cause in some sort to think no less, whatsoever some do, or may imagine to the contrary, especially some astrologers, knowing of the eclipse of the sun which we saw the same year before in our voyage thitherward, which unto them appeared very terrible. And also of a comet which began to appear but a few days before the beginning of the said sickness. But to exclude them from being the special causes of so special an accident, there are further reasons than I think fit at this present to be alleged. These their opinions I have set down the more at large, that it may appear unto you that there is good hope they may be brought through discreet dealing and government to the embracing of the truth, and consequently to honour, obey, fear, and love us.

And although some of our company towards the end of the year, shewed themselves too fierce in slaying some of the people in some towns, upon causes that on our part might easily enough have been borne withal; yet notwithstanding, because it was on their part justly deserved, the alteration of their opinions generally and for the most part concerning us is the less to be doubted. And whatsoever else they may be, by carefulness of our selves need nothing at all to be feared.

[10]Pleased; chose.

8

HERNÁN CORTÉS

Letters from Mexico

1522

The great Castilian adventurer Hernán Cortés represented the gold standard for conquistadors, and he loomed large in Ralegh's imagination. He is mentioned explicitly in the Discovery, *and, more generally, Ralegh repeatedly invokes the prospect of discovering an immense and rich*

Hernán Cortés, *Letters from Mexico*, 2nd ed., trans. and ed. Anthony Pagden, introduction by J. H. Elliott (New Haven, Conn.: Yale University Press, 1986), 99–102.

empire comparable to the one reported—and brutally subdued—by Cortés. Cortés's Cartas de relación *—official letters sent to the Habsburg court beginning in 1519 and published from 1522—provided Europe with its first glimpse of the magnificent Aztec Empire. Ralegh was hardly alone in hoping to replicate Cortés's deeds, even if he imagined doing so without the violence and "tyranny" exhibited by Cortés. The early description of Tenochtitlán (present-day Mexico City) also had the effect of making Europeans recognize the sophistication and riches of the great Mesoamerican polities of the period. The lands and peoples of Mexico now fell under Habsburg jurisdiction, and in this excerpt, Cortés details the strange and marvelous things produced in the name of the Aztec emperor Montezuma, which now came into the possession of the Holy Roman emperor Charles V. This passage highlights the immense power of the Aztec ruler, the newly extended imperial reach of the Habsburg emperor, and, implicitly, the widely praised glory of the latter's servant, Hernán Cortés.*

I spoke one day with Mutezuma[1] and told him that Your Highness had need of gold for certain works You had ordered to be done. I asked him therefore to send some of his people together with some Spaniards to the countries and dwellings of those chiefs who had submitted themselves, to ask them to render to Your Majesty some part of what they owned, for, as well as the need which Your Highness had, they were now beginning to serve Your Highness, who would have thereby higher regard for their good intentions. I also asked him to give me something of what he possessed, for I wished to send it to Your Majesty, as I had sent the gold and other things with the messengers. Later he asked for the Spaniards he wished to send, and by twos and fives dispatched them to many provinces and cities, whose names I do not remember, because I have lost my writings, and they were so many and so varied, and, moreover, because some of them were eighty and a hundred leagues from the great city of Temixtitan.[2] With them he sent some of his own people, and ordered them to go to the chiefs of those provinces and cities and tell them I demanded that each of them should give me a certain quantity of gold. And so it was done, and all the chiefs to whom he sent gave very fully of all that was asked of them, both in jewelry and in ingots and gold and silver sheets, and other things which they had.

[1] Montezuma, the Aztec ruler.
[2] Tenochtitlán.

When all was melted down that could be, Your Majesty's fifth came to more than 32,400 *pesos de oro*, exclusive of the gold and silver jewelry, and the featherwork and precious stones and many other valuable things which I designated for Your Holy Majesty and set aside; all of which might be worth a hundred thousand ducats or more. All these, in addition to their intrinsic worth, are so marvelous that considering their novelty and strangeness they are priceless; nor can it be believed that any of the princes of this world, of whom we know, possess any things of such high quality.

And lest Your Highness should think all this is an invention, let me say that all the things of which Mutezuma has ever heard, both on land and in the sea, they have modeled, very realistically, either in gold and silver or in jewels or feathers, and with such perfection that they seem almost real. He gave many of these for Your Highness, without counting other things which I drew for him and which he had made in gold, such as holy images, crucifixes, medallions, ornaments, necklaces and many other of our things. Of the silver Your Highness received a hundred or so marks, which I had the natives make into plates, both large and small, and bowls and cups and spoons which they fashioned as skillfully as we could make them understand. In addition to this, Mutezuma gave me many garments of his own, which even considering that they were all of cotton and not silk were such that in all the world there could be none like them, nor any of such varied and natural colors or such workmanship. Amongst them were very marvelous clothes for men and women, and there were bedspreads which could not have been compared even with silk ones. There were also other materials, like tapestries which would serve for hallways and churches, and counterpanes for beds, of feathers and cotton, in various colors and also very wonderful, and many other things which as there are so many and so varied I do not know how to describe them to Your Majesty.

He also gave me a dozen blowpipes, such as he uses, whose perfection I am likewise unable to describe to Your Highness, for they were all painted in the finest paints and perfect colors, in which were depicted all manner of small birds and animals and trees and flowers and several other things. Round their mouthpieces and muzzles was a band of gold a span in depth, and round the middle another, finely decorated. He also gave me pouches of gold mesh for the pellets and told me that he would give me pellets of gold as well. He also gave me some gold bullet-molds and many other things which are too numerous to describe.

Most Powerful Lord, in order to give an account to Your Royal Excellency of the magnificence, the strange and marvelous things of this great city of Temixtitan and of the dominion and wealth of this Mutezuma, its ruler, and of the rites and customs of the people, and of the order there is in the government of the capital as well as in the other cities of Mutezuma's dominions, I would need much time and many expert narrators. I cannot describe one hundredth part of all the things which could be mentioned, but, as best I can, I will describe some of those I have seen which, although badly described, will, I well know, be so remarkable as not to be believed, for we who saw them with our own eyes could not grasp them with our understanding. But Your Majesty may be certain that if my account has any fault it will be, in this as in all else of which I give account to Your Highness, too short rather than too long, because it seems to me right that to my Prince and Lord I should state the truth very clearly without adding anything which might be held to embroider it or diminish it.

Before I begin to describe this great city and the others which I mentioned earlier, it seems to me, so that they may be better understood, that I should say something of Mesyco,[3] which is Mutezuma's principal domain and the place where this city and the others which I have mentioned are to be found. This province is circular and encompassed by very high and very steep mountains, and the plain is some seventy leagues in circumference: in this plain there are two lakes which cover almost all of it, for a canoe may travel fifty leagues around the edges. One of these lakes is of fresh water and the other, which is the larger, is of salt water. A small chain of very high hills which cuts across the middle of the plain separates these two lakes. At the end of this chain a narrow channel which is no wider than a bowshot between these hills and the mountains joins the lakes. They travel between one lake and the other and between the different settlements which are on the lakes in their canoes without needing to go by land. As the salt lake rises and falls with its tides as does the sea, whenever it rises, the salt water flows into the fresh as swiftly as a powerful river, and on the ebb the fresh water passes to the salt.

This great city of Temixtitan is built on the salt lake, and no matter by what road you travel there are two leagues from the main body of the city to the mainland. There are four artificial causeways leading to it, and each is as wide as two cavalry lances. The city itself is as big as Seville or Córdoba.

[3] Mexico.

A Chronology of Sir Walter Ralegh
with Key Events from the History
of Exploration (1492–1630)

1492 Christopher Columbus reaches the Caribbean, or "Indies." On subsequent voyages (1493–1502), he sails along the mainland, including the Orinoco delta.

1497–
1498 Giovanni (John) Cabot undertakes the first American voyages for the English crown.

1519–
1521 Hernán Cortés conquers the Aztec Empire (Mexico); records his deeds in a series of well-publicized letters (*relaciónes*) published from 1522.

1532 Francisco Pizarro conquers the Inca Empire of Peru.

1552 Bartolomé de Las Casas publishes *A Short Account of the Destruction of the Indies*, his sensational history of Spanish "tyrannies" in America.

1554? Ralegh born (date is uncertain) to Squire Walter Ralegh and his third wife, Katherine Champernowne Gilbert Ralegh, in Hayes Barton near Budleigh (Devon).

1558 Coronation of Queen Elizabeth I.

1568?–
1572 Ralegh likely in France, fighting in support of the French Huguenots.

1572–
1574 Ralegh likely at Oxford, in residence at Oriel College (officially registered for 1572).

1575 Ralegh transfers from Lyon's Inn to the Middle Temple, London.

1576 Ralegh publishes his first poem, a commendatory verse for George Gascoigne, in *The Steele Glas*.

1578–
1579   Ralegh participates, as captain of the *Falcon*, in Sir Humphrey Gilbert's exploration in search of the Northwest Passage.

1580–
1581   Ralegh performs military service in Ireland and conducts diplomatic missions to London.

1582   Ralegh joins an important diplomatic mission to the Netherlands with the earl of Leicester.

1583   Ralegh receives the first of many lucrative grants from the queen, a patent to license wine; also given the use of Durham House in London.

1584   Ralegh elected to Parliament for Devon (seat held for most of the next two decades); receives customs duties on wool exports and a patent for the discovery of foreign land; begins his sponsorship of the Roanoke voyages (continues through 1587).

Richard Hakluyt writes his *Discourse of Western Planting* to encourage British colonization in America.

1585   Ralegh knighted by the queen; appointed steward of the duchy of Cornwall and lord warden of the Stanneries (tin mines).

1586   Ralegh receives valuable land grant in Munster, Ireland.

1587   Ralegh appointed lord lieutenant of Cornwall and deputy lieutenant of Devon; elevated to captain of the guard; launches the warship *Ark Ralegh* (later renamed *Ark Royal*); appointed to the Council of War; sponsors final Roanoke voyage.

1588   Attack of the Spanish Armada, in which Ralegh serves in both Cornwall and the English Channel.

Thomas Harriot publishes *A Brief and True Report of the New Found Land of Virginia*.

1589   Ralegh back in Ireland, where he meets Edmund Spenser; Spenser returns with him to London and presents *The Faerie Queene* at court.

Ralegh transfers his Virginia colony to syndicated ownership.

Hakluyt publishes the first edition of *The Principall Navigations* (expanded edition, 1598–1600).

1590   Ralegh composes two dedicatory poems for *The Faerie Queene*.

1591?   Ralegh marries Elizabeth Throckmorton (date is uncertain).

1591   Ralegh prepares fleet to resist expected Spanish attack; publishes *Revenge* tract to praise the heroism of his captured kinsman Sir Richard Grenville.

1592   *January*: Queen bestows Sherborne Castle on Ralegh.

March 26: Ralegh's first son, Damerei, born.

July: Ralegh rapidly loses favor with the queen and is imprisoned in the Tower of London.

September: Ralegh exiled from London.

1593   *November*: Ralegh's second son, Walter ("Wat"), baptized.

1594   Letters of marque granted to Ralegh authorizing privateering against Spain.

1595   *February–September*: Ralegh's first voyage to Guiana.

October?: Ralegh composes *The Discovery of Guiana* upon his return to London.

1596   Ralegh publishes the *Discovery.*

Raid on Cádiz, in which Ralegh performs heroically and badly injures his leg.

Lawrence Keymis's voyage to Guiana and publication of his *Second Voyage.*

1597   Ralegh reconciles with the queen; resumes his duties as captain of the guard; commands squadron in the Islands Voyage and attack on Spain.

1600   Ralegh appointed governor of Jersey.

1603   *March 24*: Queen Elizabeth dies; James I ascends to the English throne, and Ralegh loses his wine-licensing patent, his offices (captain of the guard, lord lieutenant of Cornwall, governor of Jersey), and the use of Durham House.

July: Ralegh arrested.

November: Ralegh convicted of high treason.

December: Ralegh's death sentence commuted to life in prison.

1603–
1616   Ralegh confined in the Tower of London.

1605   *February*: Ralegh's son Carew baptized.

1607   Virginia Company sends 144 men and boys to establish Jamestown, to the north of the former Roanoke colony (near the Chesapeake Bay).

1614   Ralegh publishes *The History of the World* to much acclaim.

1616   Warrant issued for Ralegh's release so that preparations can be made for his second voyage to Guiana.

1617   Ralegh's second voyage to Guiana, with privateering and bad weather en route.

1618 Ralegh's exploration of Guiana, under Keymis's command.

January: Wat dies.

March: Keymis commits suicide.

Spring: Ralegh returns to England by way of Ireland.

July: Order issued for Ralegh's arrest.

August: Ralegh fails to escape to France.

October 29: Ralegh executed for treason.

1620 English Puritans land at Plymouth to establish their first settlement in New England.

1630 Massachusetts Bay Colony established, followed by the great migration of Puritans to settlements in North America.

Questions for Consideration

1. Why did Ralegh wish to explore Guiana? What were his chief expressed motives, and what might have been his less explicitly articulated interests? What did he expect to find? How does the expression of his motives in the published book the *Discovery* compare with those in the unpublished manuscript "Of the Voyage for Guiana" (Document 6)?

2. Why would the history of Spanish exploration in Guiana and the surrounding region have been of such importance to Ralegh? More generally, what role do the earlier Spanish conquistadors play in Ralegh's narrative? What place did Spanish imperial history have in the development of English expansion?

3. What impression does Ralegh give of the indigenous inhabitants of Guiana? What does he seem to think of English (versus Spanish) relations with the inhabitants of America? What conceptions would Ralegh—or Thomas Harriot (Document 7)—have had of non-Europeans before their bona fide contact with Indians? Do their writings show evidence of any adjustment of these ideas?

4. Is it possible to get the indigenous side of the story of European-American "encounter" from English documents? If so, how? How might the engravings and maps in Figures 5–11 have contributed to Europeans' image of the Indians? What does Ralegh's narrative ultimately tell us about the inhabitants "discovered" in Guiana?

5. How did Ralegh respond to the natural world of Guiana? In the *Discovery*, what kind of interest does he express in the natural environment? How, more generally, was the environment addressed in other premodern documents? Is there a distinct literary mode used when describing nature?

6. In what light does the *Discovery* present its author? How does it serve Ralegh's program of "self-fashioning"? How does the use of rhetorical language and literary imagery serve Ralegh's purposes, and how does the language of the prose narrative compare with Ralegh's efforts as a poet (Document 2)? How does the literary representation of Ralegh compare with the visual representations included here (Figures 1–4)?

7. Consider the lot of an English soldier-sailor in the early modern tropics. What were the challenges of voyages of "discovery," and what were the potential rewards? What were the "temptations" of discovery and what were the day-in-the-life realities of life at sea and in the American jungle? Do you think the effort would have been worth the results?

8. How did Ralegh perceive his voyage in the context of English imperial aims? Does he deserve the title "father of the British Empire," which some historians have granted him? Are there indications in his text of an English colonial policy? Does the *Discovery* ultimately narrate a personal or a national story? What role did Queen Elizabeth play in the "discovery" of Guiana?

Selected Bibliography

EDITIONS OF THE *DISCOVERY* AND OTHER MAJOR WORKS BY RALEGH

Harlow, V. T. *Ralegh's Last Voyage.* London: Argonaut Press, 1932. An excellent overview of the final voyage, with manuscript material and the 1650 pamphlet *Sir Walter Rawleigh His Apologie for His Voyage to Guiana.*

Latham, Agnes, and Joyce Youings, eds. *The Letters of Sir Walter Ralegh.* Exeter: University of Exeter Press, 1999.

Lorimer, Joyce, ed. *Sir Walter Ralegh's Discoverie of Guiana.* Hakluyt Society Publications, 3rd ser., 15. Aldershot: Ashgate, 2006. A revised scholarly edition with new manuscript material incorporated.

Ralegh, Sir Walter. *The Discovery of the Large, Rich, and Beautiful Empire of Guiana, with a Relation of the Great and Golden City of Manoa.* Edited by Robert H. Schomburgk. Hakluyt Society Publications, vol. 3. London, 1848. The first modern scholarly edition.

Ralegh, Sir Walter. *The Discoverie of the Large and Bewtiful Empire of Guiana.* Edited by V. T. Harlow. London: Argonaut Press, 1928. An excellent edition, with the original text and related documents.

Ralegh, Sir Walter. *The Discoverie of the Large, Rich and Bewtiful Empyre of Guiana.* Edited by Neil L. Whitehead. American Exploration and Travel Series, vol. 77. Norman: University of Oklahoma Press, 1997. An edition particularly attentive to ethnographic matters pertaining to the indigenous population of Guiana.

Ralegh, Sir Walter. *The History of the World.* Edited by C. A. Patrides. Philadelphia: Temple University Press, 1971. The most accessible edition of Ralegh's other major work, which was originally published in 1614.

Rudick, Michael, ed. *The Poems of Sir Walter Ralegh: A Historical Edition.* Renaissance English Text Society, 7th ser., 23. Tempe: Arizona Center for Medieval and Renaissance Studies, 1999.

RELATED PRIMARY SOURCES

Anonymous. *Newes of Sir Walter Rauleigh, with the True Description of Guiana.* London: H. G. for I. Wright, 1618. A defense of Ralegh and the Guiana voyages, with a more general call to imperial arms.

Cortés, Hernán. *Letters from Mexico*, 2nd ed. Translated and edited by Anthony Pagden. Introduction by J. H. Elliott. New Haven, Conn.: Yale University Press, 2001.

Keymis, Lawrence. *A Relation of the Second Voyage to Guiana*. 1596. Reprint, New York: Da Capo Press, 1968. Details Keymis's follow-up voyage and provides other supporting materials, including George Chapman's poem "De Guiana, carmen epicum."

Las Casas, Bartolomé de. *A Short Account of the Destruction of the Indies*. Translated by Nigel Griffin. Introduction by Anthony Pagden. New York: Penguin, 1992.

Mancall, Peter, ed. *Travel Narratives from the Age of Discovery: An Anthology*. Oxford: Oxford University Press, 2006.

Quinn, David Beers, ed. *The Roanoke Voyages, 1584–1590*. 2 vols. Hakluyt Society Publications, 2nd ser., 104–5. London, 1955. A comprehensive edition of documents related to the Ralegh-sponsored expeditions to Roanoke and Virginia.

BIOGRAPHIES

Aubrey, John. *Aubrey's Brief Lives*. Edited by Oliver Lawson Dick. London: Secker and Warburg, 1949. 253–60. The most influential of the contemporary biographies.

Edwards, Edward. *The Life of Sir Walter Ralegh*. 2 vols. London: Macmillan, 1868. The first full, scholarly biography, which includes a superb collection of primary documents.

Edwards, Philip. *Sir Walter Ralegh*. London: Longmans, Green, 1953. A brief overview, with special attention to literary matters.

Lacey, Robert. *Sir Walter Ralegh*. London: Weidenfeld and Nicolson, 1973. A good and highly readable account.

May, Steven W. *Sir Walter Ralegh*. Boston: Twayne, 1989. A brief overview of Ralegh's literary life.

Trevelyan, Raleigh. *Sir Walter Raleigh*. London: Allen Lane, 2002. A recent, sympathetic account written by a distant relation.

CRITICAL STUDIES

Beer, Anna R. *Sir Walter Ralegh and His Readers in the Seventeenth Century: Speaking to the People*. New York: St. Martin's, 1997. On the afterlife of Ralegh, his political achievements, and his literary works.

Fuller, Mary C. "Ralegh's Fugitive Gold: Reference and Deferral in the 'Discoverie of Guiana.'" *Representations* 33 (1991): 42–64.

Greenblatt, Stephen J. *Sir Walter Ralegh: The Renaissance Man and His Roles*. New Haven, Conn.: Yale University Press, 1973. A rich and often overlooked biography by a leading Renaissance scholar.

Hamlin, William M. "Imagined Apotheoses: Drake, Harriot, and Ralegh in the Americas." *Journal of the History of Ideas* 57, no. 3 (1996): 405–28.

Hill, Christopher. "Ralegh—Science, History, and Politics." In *Intellectual Origins of the English Revolution*, 131–224. Oxford: Oxford University Press, 1965.

Lefranc, Pierre. *Sir Walter Ralegh écrivain: l'oeuvre et les idées*. Paris: Libraire Armand Colin, 1968.

Montrose, Louis. "The Work of Gender in the Discourse of Discovery." *Representations* 33 (1991): 1–41.

Nicholl, Charles. *The Creature in the Map: A Journey to El Dorado*. London: Jonathan Cape, 1995. A modern retelling and reenactment of Ralegh's first Guiana voyage.

Oakeshott, Walter. *The Queen and the Poet*. London: Faber and Faber, 1960. A thoughtful study of Ralegh as courtier and poet.

Oakeshott, Walter. "Sir Walter Ralegh's Library." *Library*, 5th ser., 23 (December 1968): 285–327.

Quinn, David B. *Raleigh and the British Empire*, rev. ed. New York: Collier, 1962. First published 1947. A classic work in imperial history.

Racin, John. *Sir Walter Ralegh as Historian: An Analysis of the "History of the World."* Salzburg Studies in English Literature: Elizabethan and Renaissance Studies, vol. 2. Salzburg: Institut für Englische Sprache und Literatur, 1974.

Sánchez, Jean-Pierre. "'El Dorado' and the Myth of the Golden Fleece." In *The Classical Tradition and the Americas*. Edited by Wolfgang Haase and Meyer Reinhold. Berlin: Walter de Gruyter, 1993.

Schmidt, Benjamin. "Reading Ralegh's America: Texts, Books, and Readers in the Early Modern Atlantic World." In *The Atlantic World and Virginia, 1550–1624*. Edited by Peter Mancall, 454–88. Chapel Hill: University of North Carolina Press, 2007. A study of the reception of Ralegh's texts (both the *Discovery* and *History of the World*) in England and on the Continent.

Skelton, R. A. "Ralegh as Geographer." *Virginia Magazine of History and Biography* 71 (April 1963): 130–49.

Vaughan, Alden T. "Sir Walter Ralegh's Indian Interpreters, 1584–1618." *William and Mary Quarterly*, 3rd ser., 59 (2002): 341–76.

BIBLIOGRAPHIES

Armitage, Christopher M., comp. *Sir Walter Ralegh, An Annotated Bibliography*. Chapel Hill: University of North Carolina Press, 1987.

Brushfield, Thomas Nadauld. *A Bibliography of Sir Walter Raleigh Knt.*, 2nd ed. with notes revised and enlarged. 1908. Reprint, New York: Burt Franklin, 1968.

Acknowledgments (continued from p. iv)

Document 4: From *The Travels of Sir John Mandeville*, Sir John Mandeville. Translated with an introduction by Charles W. R. D. Moseley. Penguin Classics, 1983. pp. 116–18, 134–38. The translation, introduction, and notes copyright © C. W. R. D. Moseley 1983. Reproduced by permission of Penguin Books, Ltd.

Document 5: From *A Short Account of the Destruction of the Indies*, Bartolomé de Las Casas. Edited and translated by Nigel Griffin, introduction by Anthony Pagden. Penguin Classics, 1992. pp. 86–93. The translation and notes copyright © Nigel Griffin, 1992. Introduction copyright © Anthony Pagden 1992. Reproduced by permission of Penguin Books, Ltd.

Document 8: From *Letters from Mexico*, Hernán Cortés. Translated, edited, and with a new introduction by Anthony Pagden; with an introductory essay by J. H. Elliott. 99–102. Reprinted with permission of Yale University Press. All rights reserved.

Index